THE BRITISH IN INDIA

Imperialism or Trusteeship?

PROBLEMS IN EUROPEAN CIVILIZATION

UNDER THE EDITORIAL DIRECTION OF
Ralph W. Greenlaw and Dwight E. Lee†*

Other volumes in preparation

9/66

PROBLEMS IN EUROPEAN CIVILIZATION

THE BRITISH IN INDIA

Imperialism or Trusteeship?

E 70

EDITED WITH AN INTRODUCTION BY

Martin Deming Lewis

SIR GEORGE WILLIAMS UNIVERSITY, QUEBEC

D. C. HEATH AND COMPANY · BOSTON

Englewood · Indianapolis · Dallas · San Francisco · Atlanta

Table of Contents

THE POLITICAL ASPECT (I)

THE POLITICAL ASPECT (II)

TOWARD FREEDOM

Introduction

IN the shaping of the modern world, few historical processes have had greater significance than the impact of European imperialism on Asia and Africa, and the reaction and response which came in its train. The most spectacular single example of this process may be seen in the history of Britain's Indian Empire. Writing in 1942, an official British spokesman declared:

No romance can compare with the story of the handful of Englishmen . . . who, beginning as mere traders and merchant settlers, have in barely two centuries built up the majestic structure of an Imperial system under which peace, order and good government are secured for three hundred and fifty millions of human beings inhabiting what is in essence a continent of its own.[1]

One might debate this characterization of the results of British rule, but who can deny that it captures something of the inherent drama of the situation? There is no parallel in history to this story of imperial control maintained for so long, and over such a large and populous area, by a small and distant nation. To Indian nationalists, however, there was another dimension to British rule. Jawaharlal Nehru, while serving his ninth term of imprisonment in a British jail in India, wrote in 1944 that

those parts of India which have been longest under British rule are the poorest today. . . . Nearly all our major problems today have grown up during British rule and as a direct result of British policy: the princes; the minority problem; various vested interests, foreign and Indian; the lack of industry and the neglect of agriculture; the extreme backwardness in the social services; and, above all, the tragic poverty of the people.[2]

If we are to understand the significance of European expansion, it is necessary to come to some evaluation of the British impact on India. The two centuries of British rule brought changes of basic importance in Indian life. This much is beyond dispute. But the student who seeks to evaluate these changes soon finds that historians have achieved no consensus in their judgments of the character and consequences of the British *raj*. In the broadest sense, the issues in dispute might be summed up by the question: Was British rule in India destructive or creative? Was its essence the exploitation and the impoverishment of the country for the benefit of alien rulers? Or, in contrast, did British rule serve to infuse a new dynamism into a hitherto stagnant and backward society, and to lay the essential groundwork for India's ultimate modernization? Finally, is it possible that British rule was *both* destructive and creative at the same time?

It is conventional to date the beginning of British rule from the Battle of Plassey in 1757, which gave effective control of the key Indian province of Bengal to the agents of the English East India Company. Behind this lay a century and a half of increasing involvement by "John Company" in Indian affairs. The Mughal Empire had been at its peak of effectiveness in the late 16th and early 17th centuries, but after the death of the emperor Aurungzeb in 1707 it had begun to disintegrate. For some time

[1] L. S. Amery, *India and Freedom* (London, 1942), p. 21. By permission of Oxford University Press.

[2] Jawaharlal Nehru, *The Discovery of India* (New York, 1946), pp. 295, 305–6. By permission of The John Day Company, Inc., and of Asia Publishing House.

it was unclear whether the successor power would be Indian or European — Maratha or British or French. But by the early 19th century the Company had defeated its rivals and laid a secure foundation for British rule.

The expansion of the Company's authority was paralleled by changes in its role. Originally it had been concerned solely with trade. After Plassey it took on a dual character. While continuing as a trading concern, it became sovereign in fact if not in name over an ever-widening extent of Indian territory. After an initial period of confusion lasting for several decades, the Company and its agents began to be subjected to an increasing measure of Parliamentary control, particularly after the passage of Pitt's India Act in 1784. In 1813 the Company lost its legal monopoly of the Indian trade, and in 1833 it was stripped of its commercial functions, though it remained as the governing authority in British India until 1858, when power was taken over directly by the British government in the wake of the great Mutiny of the Company's Indian army the year before.

The new British "Government of India" established in 1858 continued essentially unchanged for half a century after the Mutiny. In the 20th century, however, the rising tide of Indian nationalism led to the passage by the British Parliament of three successive Indian constitutional reforms, in 1909, 1919, and 1935. These acts modified direct British rule by the introduction of an increasing degree of Indian participation in legislative and executive authority. Finally, after the Second World War, British power on the Indian sub-continent came to an end, with the partition of British India and the establishment of the two new independent states of India and Pakistan in 1947.

Thus, in a sense, we can look back today on a completed historical process. The history of the British impact on India first began seriously to be written during the course of the long controversy between Indian nationalists and defenders of British rule which preceded the achievement of Indian independence. The coming of independence has resolved one aspect of that debate, but many disputed questions remain. Is the appalling poverty of the Indian and Pakistani masses today *because of* or *in spite of* British rule? Was independence itself the fruit of patient British trusteeship, or was it the result of incessant nationalist agitation and the dramatic alteration in world power relationships which accompanied the Second World War? Did the British seek to train India for self-government, or did they seek to perpetuate their rule for as long as possible by a judicious mixture of "divide-and-rule" tactics when practical, and repression when necessary? Was the British *raj* truly "the white man's burden," in which the welfare of India was a primary concern, or was the main test of British policy the benefit which would accrue to Britain herself?

Obviously, it is difficult to generalize about anything as complex as the political, social, and economic effects of two centuries of history. It may facilitate our task, however, if we begin with some broad observations:

(1) The British first came to India in the era of the mercantilist empires and trading companies of the 17th and 18th centuries. Their rule lasted through the era of the "new imperialism" of the late 19th and early 20th centuries. Thus it spans the two great periods of European overseas expansion, as well as the intervening period in the first half of the 19th century when "anti-imperialist" sentiments and policies were generally in vogue.

(2) During these years Britain's own economic life underwent momentous changes. The traditional concept of a British "industrial revolution" between, say, 1770 and 1830 has been criticized by some historians,[3] but there is no question that these years were marked both by a transformation in the nature of the British textile industry and by a massive shift in the

[3] See Philip A. M. Taylor (ed.), *The Industrial Revolution in Britain: Triumph or Disaster?* in this same series.

character of Britain's foreign trade. As we shall see, some writers have considered these developments to be intimately related to the development of British rule in India. England's 19th-century role as "the workshop of the world," and, increasingly, as a major source of overseas capital investment must also be analyzed in relationship to her Indian Empire.

(3) Similarly, there were great changes in the British political and social scene. The rise of an industrial bourgeoisie in the early 19th century and the enfranchisement of the middle classes by the great Reform Bill of 1832 created a situation quite different from that which had prevailed domestically in Britain during the heyday of the "unreformed Parliament" in the first half century or so after the Battle of Plassey. When we consider the political impact of Britain on India, however, it is equally important to remember that despite the gradual democratization of British politics by the 1867 and 1884 Reform Bills, it was not until 1918 that the House of Commons was chosen by universal manhood suffrage.

(4) The technological developments which accompanied the economic and social changes of the 19th century were important in their own right. We must not forget that the British became rulers in India in the age of sailing ships and the long voyage around the southern tip of Africa. The steamship, the railroad, and the telegraph made possible a kind of relationship between Britain and India that would have been inconceivable in the days of Robert Clive and Warren Hastings. It can be argued that the opening of the Suez Canal in 1869 was more decisive than any of the conventional political turning points in British-Indian history, because it laid the basis for the integration of the Indian economy into a true world market.

(5) The expansion of British authority over the Indian sub-continent was a prolonged process lasting for almost a century, and India itself was by no means a homogeneous unit. Necessarily the nature of the British impact varied somewhat from one part of the country to another.

(6) As we have seen, the forms of British rule in India underwent numerous changes in the years between 1757 and 1947. There were also significant changes in the policies pursued in such important areas as finance, tariff and trade regulation, land policy (including the question of the land revenue, or land tax), famine relief, education, etc. Where the initial policies were admittedly deleterious to Indian interests, some writers have felt that the British deserve credit for correcting their mistakes. Others, looking at the same instances, have focused on the cumulative and continuing effects of the original policies even after they had been abandoned.

(7) Just as the nature of British rule was itself changing and developing, so too was the character of the Indian reaction and response. To a significant degree the modern Indian nationalist movement was itself a product of British rule, as well as a reaction against it. There is a world of difference between the anti-British revolt of the Company's sepoy army in 1857, supported by some of the Indian princes, and the protestations of loyalty to the Queen which were heard at the formation of the Indian National Congress in 1885. It is hardly necessary to add that the contrast is almost as great between the early Congress, with its limited and "moderate" program, and the mass movement which it became in the 1920's and 1930's, denouncing British rule and demanding immediate independence.

(8) It would be a gross oversimplification to suggest that there are just two distinct and opposing views of British rule in India, a "British interpretation" on the one side, an "Indian interpretation" on the other. If many Englishmen have written in defense and justification of their rule, almost from the beginning there were others who were sharply critical. While many of these criticisms were never translated into changes in Government policy, they form a significant element in the Brit-

ish record which cannot be overlooked. Indeed, the charges of these British critics have played a vital role in the Indian nationalist analysis of British rule. Similarly, there have been significant differences in Indian attitudes. While the Indian National Congress was unquestionably the most important manifestation of nationalist opinion, it was by no means the only such expression. Individual Indians, and other Indian organizations, often held views which differed markedly from the position of the Congress.

There are many complex problems in attempting to weigh the consequences of British rule. Consider, for example, the following discussion of India's agrarian and famine problem, written at the beginning of the 20th century by an Englishman who had served for thirty-five years as a member of the higher bureaucracy of the British Government in India, the Indian Civil Service, whose father and grandfather had served before him for sixty years, and whose son was also a member of that Service:

There is no department of the Government to which more incessant and continuous attention is devoted than the administration and collection of the land tax. In no particular are we more ready to contrast British rule with Mogul rule so largely in our own favour as in our dealings with the land. We point to our equitable assessments as enhancing the value of landed property, to our agricultural experiments as increasing its productiveness, and to the benign protection of the British Government as enabling the ryot [peasant] and his family to enjoy the fruits of their toil in unmolested quiet. But there is not one of these beliefs which is not delusive. Our dealings with the land have been more destructive of all ancient proprietary rights than were the old methods which preceded our own. Our rigid and revolutionary methods of exacting the land revenue have reduced the peasantry to the lowest extreme of poverty and wretchedness, and the procedure of our settlement courts has been the means of laying upon them burdens heavier than any they endured in former times. Famine is now more frequent than formerly and more severe, and it is the irony of fate that our statute-book is swollen with measures of relief in favour of the victims whom our administrative system has impoverished.[4]

This statement is interesting as an example of the British criticism of British rule to which we have already referred. (Needless to say, the charges it makes have not been generally accepted by British opinion, though they are similar to the views of most Indian nationalist writers.) But it is equally interesting for the way in which it links together the problems of land revenue policy on the one hand, and famine relief and legislation for the protection of cultivators' rights on the other. If the British *raj* can take credit for ameliorative measures, should it also be charged with responsibility for creating the conditions requiring relief? Or were other factors — the growth of population under the *Pax Britannica,* perhaps — the basic causes of the poverty of the Indian peasant?

Within the brief scope of this volume, it is impossible to give any full presentation of the many controversial issues in the record of British rule. Rather, it is our purpose to illustrate the major themes in dispute as an introduction to further study.

The opening selection is from Romesh Dutt, an outstanding figure in the early period of Indian nationalism. Writing at the beginning of the 20th century, Dutt argued that the desperate poverty of his country was directly traceable to the policies which had been followed during the preceding century and a half of British rule. The moderate character of Dutt's political proposals, however, stands in striking contrast to his indictment of economic policy. As a representative of the Westernized intelligentsia which dominated the Indian National Congress in pre-World War I years, Dutt firmly believed in the advan-

[4] Sir Henry Cotton, K. C. S. I., M. P., *New India, or India in Transition* (revised and enlarged edition; London, 1907), p. 83. By permission of Routledge & Kegan Paul, Ltd.

tage to India of her connection with the British Empire. While he was critical of much that the British had done, he was confident that the necessary reforms would be instituted if only public opinion in England could be made aware of India's plight.

The very tone of the excerpt which follows may suggest to the student one reason for the widening gap between Indian nationalism and the British Government in later years. During the height of the nationalist agitation in the early 1930's, a prominent British historian, Sir John A. R. Marriott, sought to review Britain's record in India. Admitting that there might have been some errors in judgment, he concluded that these had been due "less to a deficiency in goodwill than to an excess of benevolence." In his insistence that "our task in India is not yet accomplished," Marriott struck a note which was often heard from British spokesmen in the years before the Second World War.

Meanwhile, as the nationalist movement grew in strength, its critique of British rule was developed and expanded as well. A mature version of this critique is expressed in an excerpt from Jawaharlal Nehru's book, *The Discovery of India,* written during the enforced leisure of imprisonment in 1944. Placing the British conquest of India in a broader perspective of Indian and world history, Nehru argued that the British indeed had been agents of progress, but quite unconscious agents. By their conscious policies, he charged, they had "encouraged and consolidated the position of the socially reactionary groups in India, and opposed all those who worked for political and social change." Thus, British rule had served not only to exploit and impoverish India, but also to retard and arrest such progressive tendencies as existed within Indian society itself.

A markedly different view has been taken by Sir Reginald Coupland. His re-statement of "the British case," published in 1945, stressed the benefits of peace, order, and good government which the British had brought to India. British rule, he claimed, was responsible for much material and economic development; Indian poverty was the inevitable result of backward social customs and a high birth-rate. Britain had been training India for self-government; this goal would soon be realized.

The final excerpt in this first group of selections sets the nationalist critique in the framework of Marxist interpretation. R. Palme Dutt (who should not be confused with Romesh Dutt) argues that the history of British imperialism in India must be viewed in terms of three major periods, each with its characteristic form of exploitation, corresponding respectively to the eras of mercantile capitalism, industrial capitalism, and finance capitalism in England.

Two excerpts in the next section offer evaluations of the economic impact of British rule on Indian society. An American economic historian, Daniel Thorner, considers the most significant change to be the transformation of the rural economy which resulted from the introduction of new land systems and the development of commercial agriculture. Adopting a somewhat different emphasis, a recent British writer, Barbara Ward, suggests that British rule "launched but did not complete the processes of economic modernization." She attributes this result to the pervasive influence of *laissez-faire* doctrines, which she feels were not appropriate in the Indian context.

The third and fourth groups of selections are intended to illustrate contrasting interpretations of the political aspect of British rule. L. S. S. O'Malley argues that British rule was exercised in the spirit of trusteeship. Beginning as a benevolent despotism, it gradually evolved in the direction of responsible government on the British parliamentary pattern, culminating in the Government of India Act of 1935. O'Malley's analysis is followed by a selection from an American writer, Kate L. Mitchell, who examines the mechanisms of British rule from the standpoint of Indian nationalism. India, she argues, "stands as perhaps the greatest monument to British skill in devising administrative techniques for preserving control over a vast, alien, and frequently hostile population."

No analysis of British rule in India can be complete without some consideration of the role of Hindu-Muslim relations in the political history of British India. A central element of the Indian nationalist critique was the charge that the British had fostered dissension between the two main religious communities in pursuance of "divide-and-rule" tactics. Although the Indian National Congress was predominantly Hindu in composition, it had the support of many Muslims as well in its demand for a united, independent India which would be a secular, not a religious, state. After the Muslim League formulated its demand for Pakistan in 1940, however, it won increasing support among Indian Muslims for the view that the Muslim minority actually constituted a separate nation, entitled to its own Islamic state. In the end, the transfer of power in 1947 involved the partition of British India and the creation of two successor states.

To what degree, if at all, was British policy responsible for intensifying communal antagonism? Reginald Coupland sets forth the view that the British were impartial arbiters, concerned only with guaranteeing that the rights of minorities should be respected. Rama Nand Aggarwala, an Indian constitutional historian, claims in contrast that the British favored Hindus as against Muslims during the years when the British were supplanting Muslim rulers in 18th- and early 19th-century India, but reversed their policy in the late 19th century and early 20th century as a means of countering the rising tide of Indian nationalism. Finally, H. N. Brailsford, a British critic of imperialism, approaches the issue from the standpoint not of motives but of results, and suggests that the historian of the future "will have to consider not merely what we said but what we omitted to say."

The final group of selections has for its theme India's progress towards independence and partition. In the first excerpt E. W. R. Lumby, a British historian, examines the interaction of Indian nationalism and British policy and suggests some reasons why British rule in India came to an end when it did. This is followed by a selection from an American scholar, W. Norman Brown, which offers an analysis of the complex sequence of events which culminated in partition. The concluding selection is by an Indian historian and diplomat, K. M. Panikkar, who attempts to evaluate the lasting significance for world history of the period of Western dominance in Asia.

The selections which have been presented raise many controversial questions. In some instances there is general agreement as to the facts, but marked disagreement over their significance. In other cases the facts themselves are in dispute. In still others, the root of the controversy lies in differences of outlook and approach. Each student must find his own path to historical understanding. He must weigh evidence, analyze arguments, and reach his own conclusions. The excerpts in this booklet offer no more than an introduction to one of the most complex problems with which the historian can be concerned, the interaction of two civilizations. The student who wishes to pursue it further might well begin by reading the entire volumes from which these selections have been taken. Other suggestions for additional reading are given at the back of this booklet. Beyond this, it would be well to remember that there is much original research yet to be done, and that much of it will be done by the men and women who today are just beginning their historical studies.

[NOTE: Footnotes generally have been omitted from the selections which follow, except where they are necessary for clarity or where they make a substantial contribution to the author's argument.]

The Conflict of Opinion

"What are the causes of this intense poverty and these repeated famines in India? . . . In many ways, the sources of national wealth in India have been narrowed under British rule. India in the eighteenth century was a great manufacturing country as well as a great agricultural country, and the products of the Indian loom supplied the markets of Asia and Europe."

— ROMESH DUTT

"The English in India have been confronted by a unique problem. That the attempt to solve it should have revealed some errors of judgement was inevitable; but those errors have been due less to a deficiency in goodwill than to an excess of benevolence. . . ."

— SIR JOHN A. R. MARRIOTT

"One remarkable contradiction meets us at every turn in considering the record of British rule in India. The British became dominant in India, and the foremost power in the world, because they were the heralds of the new big-machine industrial civilization. They represented a new historic force which was going to change the world, and were thus, unknown to themselves, the forerunners and representatives of change and revolution. And yet they deliberately tried to prevent change, except in so far as this was necessary to consolidate their position and help them in exploiting the country and its people to their own advantage."

— JAWAHARLAL NEHRU

"Since the days when Burke told them that they had a duty to do in India, the British people have certainly tried to do it. . . . There have been shortcomings, of course, and blunders; but it is the general British belief, and it has become part of the British national tradition, that the record of the Raj, though it has one or two black pages, is on the whole a record of which the British people have sober reason to be proud."

— SIR REGINALD COUPLAND

"The British conquest of India . . . led to the most drastic changes in the Indian way of life of which we have record. The most fundamental of these changes was the disintegration of the older structure of the village community, partly as a result of new land systems, and partly as a result of the spread of commercial agriculture."

— DANIEL THORNER

"Britain's impact on the Indian economy illustrates in the clearest and most sustained way the general rule that, outside the Atlantic area, Western colonialism and Western investment launched but did not complete the processes of economic modernization. . . ."

— BARBARA WARD

"Was, in fact, any synthesis possible between the static ideas of the East and the progressive ideas of the West? The position of the British, faced with this dilemma, has aptly been compared with that of men forced to make their watches keep time in two longitudes, neither too fast to endanger security nor too slow to impede progress."

— L. S. S. O'MALLEY

"Britain has ruled India for more than 150 years, and not the least remarkable thing about that rule is that it has been accomplished with such a relatively small administrative force. . . . India stands as perhaps the greatest monument to British skill in devising administrative techniques for preserving control over a vast, alien, and frequently hostile population."

— KATE L. MITCHELL

"There is a view generally held by many European writers that the changes brought about in Asia by the contact with Europe are superficial and will, with the disappearance of European political authority, cease to count as time goes on. . . . This point of view would seem to be based on a superficial reading of history. . . . The changes that have been brought about in Asian life by the contact with Europe are radical and far-reaching, and will not disappear as many observers are inclined to think with the rise of a new Asian sentiment."

— K. M. PANIKKAR

THE PROBLEM OUTLINED

The five readings in this first section include two selections from Indian nationalist writers, two from British historians, and one from an English Marxist of part Indian descent. They illustrate not only the contrast between British and Indian interpretations, but also the way the interpretations on both sides have tended to change as the nationalist movement developed.

The Nationalist Critique

ROMESH DUTT

Born in Calcutta, Romesh Dutt (1848–1909) left home at the age of nineteen to travel to England for study. He was one of the first Indians to take the examination at London for the Indian Civil Service, receiving his appointment in 1871. After twenty-six years of service, he resigned from the I.C.S. in 1897 to devote himself to the furtherance of the nationalist cause. From 1898 to 1904 he was Lecturer in Indian History at University College, London, returning to India in 1899 to preside over the fifteenth annual session of the Indian National Congress. In the last five years of his life he served first as revenue minister and then as prime minister of the Indian princely state of Baroda. He was the author of numerous historical works in both English and Bengali, the most important being his *Economic History of India under Early British Rule* (1901) and *Economic History of India in the Victorian Age* (1903). These two books may well be considered the foundation-stone of the Indian nationalist school of historical interpretation. The selection which follows is taken from the preface to the former work.

ENGLISHMEN can look back on their work in India, if not with unalloyed satisfaction, at least with some legitimate pride. They have conferred on the people of India what is the greatest human blessing — Peace. They have introduced Western Education, bringing an ancient and civilised nation in touch with modern thought, modern sciences, modern institutions and life. They have built up an Administration which, though it requires reform with the progress of the times, is yet strong and efficacious. They have framed wise laws, and have established Courts of Justice, the purity of which is as absolute as in any country on the face of the earth. These are results which no honest critic of British rule in India regards without high admiration.

On the other hand, no open-minded Englishman contemplates the material condition of the people of India under British rule with equal satisfaction. The poverty of the Indian population at the present day is unparalleled in any civilised country; the famines which have desolated India within the last quarter of the nineteenth century are unexampled in their extent and inten-

From Romesh Dutt, *The Economic History of India under Early British Rule* (7th ed.; London, 1950), pp. v–xxi. By permission of Routledge & Kegan Paul, Ltd.

sity in the history of ancient or modern times. By a moderate calculation, the famines of 1877 and 1878, of 1889 and 1892, of 1897 and 1900, have carried off fifteen millions of people. The population of a fair-sized European country has been swept away from India within twenty-five years. A population equal to half of that of England has perished in India within a period which men and women, still in middle age, can remember.

What are the causes of this intense poverty and these repeated famines in India? Superficial explanations have been offered one after another, and have been rejected on close examination. It was said that the population increased rapidly in India, and that such increase must necessarily lead to famines; it is found on inquiry that the population has never increased in India at the rate of England, and that during the last ten years it has altogether ceased to increase. It was said that the Indian cultivators were careless and improvident, and that those who did not know how to save when there was plenty, must perish when there was want; but it is known to men who have lived all their lives among these cultivators, that there is not a more abstemious, a more thrifty, a more frugal race of peasantry on earth. It was said that the Indian money-lender was the bane of India, and by his fraud and extortion kept the tillers of the soil in a chronic state of indebtedness; but the inquiries of the latest Famine Commission have revealed that the cultivators of India are forced under the thraldom of money-lenders by the rigidity of the Government revenue demand. It was said that in a country where the people depended almost entirely on their crops, they must starve when the crops failed in years of drought; but the crops in India, as a whole, have never failed, there has never been a single year when the food supply of the country was insufficient for the people, and there must be something wrong, when failure in a single province brings on a famine, and the people are unable to buy their supplies from neighbouring provinces rich in harvests.

Deep down under all these superficial explanations we must seek for the true causes of Indian poverty and Indian famines. The economic laws which operate in India are the same as in other countries of the world; the causes which lead to wealth among other nations lead to prosperity in India; the causes which impoverish other nations impoverish the people of India. Therefore, the line of inquiry which the economist will pursue in respect of India is the same which he adopts in inquiring into the wealth or poverty of other nations. Does agriculture flourish? Are industries and manufactures in a prosperous condition? Are the finances properly administered, so as to bring back to the people an adequate return for the taxes paid by them? Are the sources of national wealth widened by a Government anxious for the material welfare of the people? These are questions which the average Englishman asks himself when inquiring into the economic condition of any country in the world; these are questions which he will ask himself in order to ascertain the truth about India.

It is, unfortunately, a fact which no well-informed Indian official will ignore, that, in many ways, the sources of national wealth in India have been narrowed under British rule. India in the eighteenth century was a great manufacturing as well as a great agricultural country, and the products of the Indian loom supplied the markets of Asia and of Europe. It is, unfortunately, true that the East India Company and the British Parliament, following the selfish commercial policy of a hundred years ago, discouraged Indian manufacturers in the early years of British rule in order to encourage the rising manufactures of England. Their fixed policy, pursued during the last decades of the eighteenth century and the first decades of the nineteenth, was to make India subservient to the industries of Great Britain, and to make the Indian people grow raw produce only, in order to supply material for the looms and manufactories of Great Britain. This policy was pursued with unwavering resolution and with fatal success; orders were sent out, to force Indian artisans to work in the Company's factories; commercial residents were legally vested with extensive powers over villages and communities of Indian weavers; prohibitive tariffs excluded Indian silk and cotton goods from England; English goods were admitted into India free of duty or on payment of a nominal duty.

The British manufacturer, in the words of the historian, H. H. Wilson, "employed the arm of political injustice to keep down and ultimately strangle a competitor with whom he could not have contended on equal terms"; millions of Indian artisans lost their earnings; the population of India lost one great source of their wealth. It is a painful episode in the history of British rule in India; but it is a story which has to be told to explain the economic condition of the Indian people, and their present helpless dependence on agriculture. The invention of the power-loom in Europe completed the decline of the Indian industries; and when in recent years the power-loom was set up in India, England once more acted towards India with unfair jealousy. An excise duty has been imposed on the production of cotton fabrics in India which disables the Indian manufacturer from competing with the manufacturer of Japan and China, and which stifles the new steam-mills of India.

Agriculture is now virtually the only remaining source of national wealth in India, and four-fifths of the Indian people depend on agriculture. But the Land Tax levied by the British Government is not only excessive, but, what is worse, it is fluctuating and uncertain in many provinces. . . . It is true that the British Government only followed the precedent of the previous Mahomedan rulers, who also claimed an enormous Land Tax. But the difference was this, that what the Mahomedan rulers claimed they could never fully realise; what

the British rulers claimed they realised with rigour. The last Mahomedan ruler of Bengal, in the last year of his administration (1764), realised a land revenue of £817,553; within thirty years the British rulers realised a land revenue of £2,680,000 in the same Province. In 1802 the Nawab of Oudh ceded Allahabad and some other rich districts in Northern India to the British Government. The land revenue which had been claimed by the Nawab in these ceded districts was £1,352,347; the land revenue which was claimed by the British rulers within three years of the cession was £1,682,306. In Madras, the Land Tax first imposed by the East India Company was one-half the gross produce of the land! In Bombay, the land revenue of the territory conquered from the Mahrattas in 1817 was £800,000 in the year of the conquest; it was raised to £1,500,000 within a few years of British rule; and it has been continuously raised since. "No Native Prince demands the rent which we do," wrote Bishop Heber in 1826, after travelling all through India, and visiting British and Native States. "A Land Tax like that which now exists in India," wrote Colonel Briggs in 1830, "professing to absorb the whole of the landlord's rent, was never known under any Government in Europe or Asia."

The people of Bengal and of Northern India gradually obtained some relief from the heavy land assessment of the early years of British rule. In Bengal the assessment was made permanent; and as it has not been raised with the extension of cultivation, it now bears (including Road and Public Work cesses [i.e., taxes—ED.], which have been since imposed on the rental) a ratio of about 35 per cent on the rental. In Northern India the assessment was not made permanent, but it was reduced to slightly over 50 per cent, including all cesses, in 1855. But new cesses were added; calculations were made, not on the current, but on the prospective rental, until the tax rose to close upon 60 per cent on the rental.

In Madras and Bombay things are worse.

There the Land Tax is paid generally by the cultivators of the soil, there being, in most parts of those provinces, no intervening landlords. The British Government declared its intention in 1864 of realising as Land Tax about one-half of the economic rent. But what the British Government does take as Land Tax at the present day sometimes approximates to the whole of the economic rent, leaving the cultivators little beyond the wages of their labour and the profits of their agricultural stock. The Land Tax is revised every thirty years; the cultivator does not know on what grounds it is enhanced; he has to submit to each renewed assessment, or to leave his ancestral fields and perish. This uncertainty of the Land Tax paralyses agriculture, prevents saving, and keeps the tiller of the soil in a state of poverty and indebtedness.

It will appear from the facts stated above that the Land Tax in India is not only heavy and uncertain, but that the very principle on which it is raised is different from the principle of taxation in all well-administered countries. In such countries the State promotes the accumulation of wealth, helps the people to put money into their pockets, likes to see them prosperous and rich, and then demands a small share of their earnings for the expenses of the State. In India the State virtually interferes with the accumulation of wealth from the soil, intercepts the incomes and gains of the tillers, and generally adds to its land revenue demand at each recurring settlement, leaving the cultivators permanently poor. In England, in Germany, in the United States, in France and other countries, the State widens the income of the people, extends their markets, opens out new sources of wealth, identifies itself with the nation, grows richer with the nation. In India, the State has fostered no new industries and revived no old industries for the people; on the other hand, it intervenes at each recurring land settlement to take what it considers its share out of the produce of the soil. Each new settlement in Bombay and in Madras is regarded by the people as a wrangle between them and the State as to how much the former will keep and how much the latter will take. It is a wrangle decided without any clear limits fixed by the law — a wrangle in which the opinion of the revenue officials is final, and there is no appeal to judges or Land Courts. The revenue increases and the people remain destitute.

Taxation raised by a king, says the Indian poet, is like the moisture of the earth sucked up by the sun, to be returned to the earth as fertilising rain; but the moisture raised from the Indian soil now descends as fertilising rain largely on other lands, not on India. Every nation reasonably expects that the proceeds of taxes raised in the country should be mainly spent in the country. Under the worst governments that India had in former times, this was the case. The vast sums which Afghan and Mughal Emperors spent on their armies went to support great and princely houses, as well as hundreds of thousands of soldiers and their families. The gorgeous palaces and monuments they built, as well as the luxuries and displays in which they indulged, fed and encouraged the manufacturers and artisans of India. Nobles and Commanders of the army, Subadars, Dewans, and Kazis, and a host of inferior officers in every province and every district, followed the example of the Court; and mosques and temples, roads, canals and reservoirs, attested to their wide liberality, or even to their vanity. Under wise rulers as under foolish kings, the proceeds of taxation flowed back to the people and fructified their trade and industries.

But a change came over India under the rule of the East India Company. They considered India as a vast estate or plantation, the profits of which were to be withdrawn from India and deposited in Europe. They reserved all the high appointments in India for their own nominees seeking a lucrative career in the East. They bought their merchandise out of the revenues of India, and sold it in Europe for their own profit. They vigorously exacted from India a high interest on their stock-in-trade. In one shape or another all that could be raised in India by an excessive taxation flowed to Europe, after paying for a starved administration.

The East India Company's trade was abolished in 1833, and the Company was abolished in 1858, but their policy remains. Their capital was paid off by loans which were made into an Indian Debt, on which interest is paid from Indian taxes. The empire was transferred from the Company to the Crown, but the people of India paid the purchase-money. The Indian Debt, which was £51,000,000 in 1857, rose to £97,000,000 in 1862. Within the forty years of peace which have succeeded, the Indian Debt has increased continuously, and now (1901) amounts to £200,000,000. The "Home Charges" remitted annually out of the Indian revenues to Great Britain have increased to sixteen millions. The pay of European officers in India, virtually monopolising all the higher services, comes to ten millions. One-half of the net revenues of India, which are now forty-four millions sterling, flows annually out of India. Verily the moisture of India blesses and fertilises other lands.

For one who has himself spent the best and happiest years of his life in the work of Indian administration, it is an ungracious and a painful task to dwell on the weak side of that administration, the financial and economic policy of the Indian Government. I have undertaken this duty because at the present moment the economic story of British India has to be told, and the deep-seated cause of the poverty of the Indian people has to be explained. Place any other country under the same condition, with crippled industries, with agriculture subject to a heavy and uncertain Land Tax, and with financial arrangements requiring one-half of its revenues to be annually remitted out of the country, and the most prosperous nation on earth will soon know the horrors of famine. A nation prospers if the sources of its wealth are widened, and if the proceeds of taxation are spent among the people, and for the people. A nation is impoverished if the sources of its wealth are narrowed, and the proceeds of taxation are largely remitted out of the country. These are plain, self-evident economic laws, which operate in India, as in every other country, and the Indian statesman and administrator must feel that the poverty of India cannot be removed until Indian industries are revived, until a fixed and intelligible limit is placed on the Indian Land Tax, and until the Indian revenues are more largely spent in India. . . .

"The government of a people by itself," said John Stuart Mill, "has a meaning and a reality; but such a thing as government of one people by another does not, and cannot exist. One people may keep another for its own use, a place to make money in, a human cattle-farm to be worked for the profits of its own inhabitants."

There is more truth in this strongly worded statement than appears at first sight. History does not record a single instance of one people ruling another in the interests of the subject nation. Mankind has not yet discovered any method for safeguarding the interests of a subject nation without conceding to that nation some voice in controlling the administration of their own concerns. . . .

The Empire of India was won by England before her present colonies rose to importance. And it is possible to conceive, though it may be a heresy to say it in these days, that the Empire of India will last after the British Colonies have ceased to owe allegiance to the British Crown. Colonies have been described as fruits, which ripen only to fall from the parent tree; and he will be a bold prophet who will assert that, with some addition to their present population, power, and resources, Australasia and Canada will remain under the sovereignty of Great Britain, even to the middle of the twentieth century. In India, the people honestly desire a longer connection with Great Britain, not through sentimental loyalty, but, as Lord Dufferin once said, through a sense of self-interest. They still believe that they have much to gain by being in close touch with the West, through the rule of a Western Power. They have cast in their lot with Great Britain; they have identified themselves with British rule; they honestly desire that rule to last. But they do not desire the administration to last in its present absolute and exclusive form. This form of administration, shaped by Warren Hastings and Cornwallis, and improved by Munro, Elphinstone, and Bentinck, requires some change after seventy years. Education has spread within these seventy years; educated men are a growing power in India. They demand a fair share in the higher services of their own country; they desire to have a voice in the highest Councils of the Empire. It is easy to disregard this demand, to alienate the educated and influential sections of the Indian population, to increase discontent and dissatisfaction in the country, and to weaken the Empire by continuing an exclusive rule. It would be wiser, on the other hand, to array the rising forces on the side of the Government, to make educated and influential men in India partakers in the control of the administration, to make them represent their own interests, industries, and agriculture, and to make them responsible for improving the material condition of their countrymen and the prevention of famines. To quote once more from John Stuart Mill: "It is an inherent condition of human affairs that no intention, however sincere, of protecting the interests of others, can make it safe or salutary to tie up their own hands. By their own hands only can any positive and durable improvement of their circumstances in life be worked out."

The people of India are not fond of sudden changes and revolutions. They do not ask for new constitutions, issuing like armed Minervas from the heads of legislative Jupiters. They prefer to work on lines which have already been laid down. They desire to strengthen the present Government, and to bring it more in touch with the people. They desire to see some Indian members in the Secretary of State's Council, and in the Viceroy's Executive Council, representing Indian agriculture and industries. They wish to see Indian members in an Executive Council for each Province. They wish to represent the interests of the people in the discussion of every important administrative question. They seek that the administration of the Empire and its great provinces should be conducted with the cooperation of the people.

There is a Legislative Council in each large Indian Province, and some of the members of these Councils are elected under the Act of 1892. The experiment has proved a success, and some expansion of these Legislative Councils would strengthen administration and bring it more in touch with the people. Each Indian Province is divided into twenty or thirty or more Districts, corresponding to English counties, and each District has a population of a million or more. The time has come when each District might elect its own member for the Legislative Council of the Province. A Province with thirty Districts and a population of thirty millions may fairly have thirty elected members on its Legislative Council. Each District should feel that it has some voice in the administration of the Province.

The higher services in India, which were theoretically declared open to the people in 1833, in 1853, and by Queen Victoria's famous proclamation of 1858, should be practically opened to the people, and not reserved for English boys seeking a career in the East. In the great Indian Civil Service, as well as in the Education, Engineering, Postal, Telegraph, Police, and Medical departments, Indians should find it possible to obtain high employment. We want Englishmen in all these departments, we welcome them to help us, but we do not wish them to monopolise all the higher services to the virtual exclusion of the children of the soil. . . .

These are a few of the measures which could wisely be adopted to bring the Indian

Government more in touch with the people, and to make it more popular and more efficacious for the good of the people. Isolation does not strengthen the Empire; it leads to ill-judged, unwise, and hasty measures of legislation, and spreads dissatisfaction and discontent among the people. It leads to sudden and bewildering changes in the policy of the Indian Government as a result of party government in Great Britain. It leads to increasing expenditure, and not to retrenchment, which can only be secured, as it has been secured in other countries, through the watchfulness of those who pay the taxes. It renders the administration incapable of improving the economic condition of the people, which can be improved only through the cooperation of the people themselves. It alienates the best educated, the most moderate, and the most influential sections of the Indian people, instead of making them partakers in the work of administration and responsible for the welfare of their countrymen. It impoverishes the nation and weakens the Empire.

Proudly We May Look Back

SIR JOHN A. R. MARRIOTT

Sir John A. R. Marriott (1859–1945) taught modern history at Oxford University from 1884 to 1920, and served as a Conservative member of Parliament, 1917–1922 and 1923–1929. During the course of his lifetime he wrote more than forty books on historical and political subjects, including *Makers of Modern Italy* (1889), *England since Waterloo* (1913), *The Eastern Question: A Study in European Diplomacy* (1917), and *The English in India: A Problem of Politics* (1932), from which the following selection is taken.

In thinking of her work in India Great Britain may look back proudly, but she must also anxiously look forward." So wrote a great historian of British India towards the close of the last century. This book will have been written wholly in vain if there should linger in the mind of the reader any doubt as to the truth of the first half of Hunter's proposition. Proudly we may look back. Preceding chapters, though presenting no more than an outline sketch, should at least have sufficed to show that the English in India have been confronted by a unique problem. That the attempt to solve it should have revealed some errors of judgement was inevitable; but those errors have been due less to a deficiency in goodwill than to an excess of benevolence; perhaps to some lack of imagination, perhaps to a failure adequately to appreciate the relativity of the teachings of Political Science, but above all to a genuine anxiety to share with our Indian fellow-subjects the privileges we ourselves enjoy. Macaulay's famous Minute on Education (1835) is a case in point. The educational policy he initiated is now generally admitted to have been based upon a grave error.[1] The con-

[1] The reference is to Macaulay's successful advocacy of the use of English rather than an Indian language as a medium of instruction in higher education in India. [Editor's note]

From Sir John A. R. Marriott, *The English in India: A Problem of Politics* (Oxford, 1932), pp. 301-308. By permission of The Clarendon Press.

sequences of that initial blunder have been deplorable and are not yet exhausted. But the motive which inspired the policy was generous — a desire to share with the youth of India the rich inheritance of English literature, to admit them to the storehouse of English political philosophy, to prepare them to play their part as citizens in a Commonwealth organized on the English model. The Englishman of today is less self-satisfied than were the Victorians; a series of shocks have somewhat shaken his complacency; he is no longer convinced that he possesses a monopoly of political wisdom or of aptitude for commerce. Consequently he is less certain that his duty lies in conferring English institutions upon the rest of the world, and particularly upon that large part of it for which he is immediately responsible.

But if our fathers were in error, their error was not merely pardonable but praiseworthy. There is no reason to accept as accurate the amusing description given by Mr. Wells of the Englishman's dilemma:

The English rule in India [he wrote in *The New Machiavelli*] is surely one of the most extraordinary accidents that has ever happened in history. We are there like a man who has fallen off a ladder on to the neck of an elephant and doesn't know what to do or how to get down. . . . In some manner we shall have to come out of India. We have had our chance and we have demonstrated nothing but the appalling dullness of our national imagination. We are not good enough to do anything with India.

So far from not being "good enough to do anything with India," we have been perhaps over-anxious to do good, and have thus brought upon ourselves the Nemesis of benevolence. Take social reform. No humane government could look on unmoved at some of the cruel rites practised in the name of religion by the Hindus. Yet those rites are as sacred to them as are the Sacraments of the Church to Christians. To interfere with them was to engender suspicion and provoke unrest.

Foreign critics are better able, perhaps, than Englishmen to view these things in perspective. That must be my excuse for quoting one or two of them. The Comte de Montalembert wrote in 1855 as follows:

For every man who loves his fellowman, who believes in the legitimate progress of the human race, who welcomes the increasing happiness of the many, what a consoling and marvellous spectacle is that of the English dominion in India. Its history in those regions is certainly not without stain. . . . But everything considered and allowing a large amount of evil, we may boldly affirm that history gives no example of a conquest so completely turned to the good of the vanquished.

Another Frenchman may be cited. M. Leroy-Beaulieu wrote: "La disparition d'une souveraineté européenne aux Indes serait un malheur et pour le pays et pour la civilisation en général." Such testimonies are the more remarkable when it is remembered that the countrymen of Dupleix had little reason to be over-tender in judging the countrymen of Clive.

The views of a typical American coincide with those of representative Frenchmen. Some twenty years ago President [Theodore] Roosevelt said:

The English administration of India is a greater feat than any performed under the Roman Empire. . . . Undoubtedly India is a less pleasant place than it was formerly for the heads of tyrannical states. There is now little or no room in it for the successful freebooters, chieftains and despots who lived in gorgeous splendour, while under their cruel rule the immense mass of their countrymen festered in sodden misery. But the mass of the people have been, and are, far better off than ever before, far better off than they would be now if English control were overthrown or withdrawn. Indeed, if English control were now withdrawn from India, the whole peninsula would become a chaos of blood and violence . . . every true friend of humanity should realize that the part which England has played in India has been of immeasurable advantage to India and to the honour and profit of civilization, and should feel profound satisfaction at the stability and permanence of English rule.[2]

Finally, we may quote the concise aphorism of M. Paul Boell: "The question is not whether England has a right to keep India, but rather whether she has a right to leave it."

She has clearly no right to leave it, until her task has been accomplished, and nothing would contribute more to its accomplishment than to make public proclamation of the warning uttered by one of the greatest of English proconsuls twenty years ago.

Writing at the time (1909) of the Morley-Minto reforms Lord Cromer expressed general agreement with the policy of associating Indians with ourselves in the task of administration. But he added this impressive warning.

It will be well for England, better for India, and best of all for the cause of progressive civilization in general, if it be clearly understood from the outset that, however liberal may be the concessions which have now (1909) been made, and which at any future time may be made, we have not the slightest intention of abandoning our Indian possessions and that it is highly improbable that any such intention will be entertained by our posterity. The foundation-stone of Indian reform must be the steadfast maintenance of British supremacy. . . . It may be that at some future and far distant time we shall be justified . . . in handing over the torch of progress and civilization in India to those whom we have ourselves civilized. All that can be said at present is that, until human nature entirely changes, and until racial and religious passions disappear from the face of the earth, the relinquishment of that torch would almost certainly lead to its extinction.

That warning is as timely today as when it was uttered. Recent events[3] have made it unmistakably clear that our task in India is not yet accomplished. Nothing, indeed, has done more to reveal to Englishmen and to the world the naked truth as to the Indian situation than the Round Table Conference.[4] We are forbidden to describe that Conference as a failure. Cynics might well proclaim it as having, beyond all their expectations, succeeded. All men of goodwill hoped — some of them against hope — that the Conference would discover some solution of the Communal problem.[5] It has, on the contrary, ended in a deadlock. It has indeed for the first time revealed, perhaps for the first time produced, a united front among all the minorities of India (except the Sikhs) against the arrogant pretensions of Brahmanism. As Lord Meston has admirably put it:

Behind and below all that [the Conference] has accomplished, there remains stark and unanswered the one vital question. . . . When we abandon the governing of India, to whom are we going to hand it over, to the Brahmin or to the people?

Failure to answer, nay, refusal to tackle that question has rendered wholly academic the discussion of abandonment. Even were it otherwise we could still look back proudly. British brains, British enterprise, and British capital have, in a material sense, transformed the face of India. Means of communication have been developed: innumerable bridges, over 40,000 miles of railway, 70,000 miles of metalled roads, testify to the skill and industry of British engineers. Irrigation works on a stupendous scale have brought 30,000,000 acres under cultivation, and thus greatly added to the agricultural wealth of a country which still lives mainly by agriculture. But, on the other hand, the process of industrialization has already be-

---

[2] Speech by the President of the U.S.A. at the celebration of the diamond jubilee of the Methodist Episcopal Church of Africa at New York, 17 Jan. 1909.

[3] The reference is presumably to the mass civil disobedience campaign initiated in 1930 by the Indian National Congress under the leadership of M. K. Gandhi, with the aim of securing immediate independence for India. [Editor's note]

[4] The conference of Indian and British leaders which met at London in November, 1930. [Editor's note]

[5] *I.e.*, the question of relations between Hindus and Muslims. [Editor's note]

gun. The mills of Bombay have become dangerous competitors to Lancashire, and the Indian jute industry is threatening the prosperity of Dundee. Thanks to improved sanitation (much resented by the more ignorant beneficiaries), to a higher standard of living, to irrigation, to canalization, to the development of transport, and to carefully thought-out schemes for relief work, famines, which by their regular recurrence formerly presented a perennial problem to humane administrators, have now virtually disappeared. To have conquered the menace of famine in the face of greater longevity, of diminished death-rate, and the suppression of war, is a remarkable achievement for which India is wholly indebted to British administration.

It might well happen that India, abandoned once more to her own resources, would furnish a striking vindication of the truth of Malthusian doctrine; that the "positive checks" — war, vice, misery, and disease — would again begin to operate, and that by this means the pressure of population upon subsistence would be averted. Under British rule that pressure has been averted by means less painful. The standard of living, though not high, has steadily risen; subsistence has more than kept pace with a rapid increase in population.

The material benefit accruing to India from British rule is not denied. But it is urged that good government is no substitute for self-government. There are many instances which tend to substantiate this aphorism. It is, however, extraordinarily difficult to get evidence from witnesses whose testimony would be really convincing. The beneficiaries under an alien rule are generally inarticulate. What would be the verdict of the Egyptian fellaheen, or the Indian peasants?

There are in India many gravely disquieting symptoms. But it is not easy to diagnose the nature of the disease. Is it organic or merely functional? Are the symptoms such as can be relieved by treatment, or do they call for a major surgical operation?

To change the metaphor. That there is in India a moving of the waters no impartial observer can doubt. It is equally certain that for this movement English administration has been primarily responsible. The increasingly close contact between a group of Asiatic people, naturally conservative in outlook, and a Western people rapidly advancing towards undiluted democracy, accounts by itself for much of the unrest. The confusion is deepened by the logical contradiction between the views of social reactionaries and political extremists. Economically, Mr. Gandhi would seem to be as reactionary as Mr. Ruskin, and yet is in close alliance with the Parsee capitalists of Bombay. Politically, the Congress Party demands the immediate concession of "Dominion Status." It must, however, be acknowledged that the Brahmins and Parsees have alike sat at the feet of English or Anglicized teachers. Everything goes back to the educational system. The "inverted pyramid" has come crashing to the ground. The only dangerous revolutionaries in India are those who have learnt their lesson from English textbooks.

It is undoubtedly true that a wave of "nationalism" has been sweeping over Asia. and has reached India, but that wave would have lapped the shores of India calmly, almost imperceptibly, had not the people, or some of them, already passed through many stages of preparation. Such nationalism as exists among the peoples of India is mainly the product of the policy persistently pursued by British administrators. English is in India the *lingua franca* of revolution. Dalhousie[6] began the work of material unification.

Yet, despite a century and a half of British rule, India still lacks unity. The map taught the world that there were two Indias — British India and the Indian States. The Round Table Conference has revealed the truth that there are not only two but many Indias, each divided from every other by fissures of religion, race, language, and caste.

[6] Governor-general, 1848–1856. [Editor's note]

For these things England has no responsibility. They are the fruit of the womb of History. If, then, we can look back proudly, we must look forward anxiously. Yet anxiety may be tempered with faith, with hope, and above all with charity. Many of the greatest and best and noblest of Englishmen have given their all to India. But looking back upon their lives and their work it is difficult to avoid the reflection that even the strongest of these men have been in the grip of a Power stronger than themselves. Their work has been "rough hewn," but plainly there has been a Providence that has shaped their ends. That Clive and Warren Hastings, that Wellesley and Dalhousie, that the Elphinstones and Lawrences foresaw the end towards which in fact they were moving it would be fantastic to suppose. Each and all seem to have been acting in blind obedience to Forces the strength and direction of which they themselves never perceived.

Have the scales fallen from our eyes? Are we more certain than they of the end towards which we move? Clio, the Muse of History, holds in her hand an open roll; it is not for her votaries to close it.

About the past we can be confident: we are proud of our record. The key-note of our rule has been efficiency, resting on the twin foundations of justice and power. British government in India has been strong, because it has been just, and just because it has been strong, and efficient because it has been both.

We are asked to place the government in other hands which we believe will be less just, less strong, and less efficient. It is no light thing to require an Imperial race to surrender the pride of achievement, and to sacrifice the fruits of it; to fling the India that it has nursed up to adolescence into the witches' cauldron, knowing not what will emerge therefrom. Nemesis was indeed the most impartial of goddesses, measuring out to mortals rewards and punishments. Which has our rule in India merited? Let the adjuration of a broad-minded Moslem[7] supply the answer.

Be not unjust to that nation which is ruling over you, and think on this — how upright is her rule. Of such benevolence as the English Government shows to the foreign nations under her rule there is no example in the history of the world.

[7] Sir Syed Ahmed [1817–1898], Founder of the Mohammedan College at Alighar. Quoted by Cromer [*Ancient and Modern Imperialism*].

British Rule in India

JAWAHARLAL NEHRU

As one of the great world leaders of our time, Jawaharlal Nehru (1889–   ) needs little introduction to the reader. Educated at Harrow and Cambridge in England, he rose to prominence in the Indian National Congress in the 1920's and was chosen president of the Congress in 1929, holding that office again in 1936, 1937, 1946, and 1951–1954. Since 1947 he has been prime minister of India. His *Autobiography* (1936; published in the United States in 1941 under the title *Toward Freedom*) and *The Discovery of India* (1946) were both written while he was in prison for nationalist activity. The reading which follows is taken from the latter work.

O
UR writing of India's history is perhaps resented more than anything else we have done" — so writes an Englishman well acquainted with India and her history. It is difficult to say what Indians have resented most in the record of British rule in India; the list is long and varied. But it is true that British accounts of India's history, more especially of what is called the British period, are bitterly resented. History is almost always written by the victors and conquerors and gives their view. Or, at any rate, the victors' version is given prominence and holds the field. . . .

Recent Indian history — that is, the history of the British period — is so connected with present-day happenings that the passions and prejudices of today powerfully influence our interpretation of it. Englishmen and Indians are both likely to err, though their errors will lie in opposite directions. Far the greater part of the records and papers out of which history takes shape and is written comes from British sources and inevitably represents the British point of view. The very circumstances of defeat and disruption prevented the Indian side of the story from being properly recorded, and many of the records that existed suffered destruction during the great revolt of 1857.

* * *

Looking back over [the 18th century], it almost seems that the British succeeded in dominating India by a succession of fortuitous circumstances and lucky flukes. With remarkably little effort, considering the glittering prize, they won a great empire and enormous wealth which helped to make them the leading power in the world. It seems easy for a slight turn in events to have taken place which would have dashed their hopes and ended their ambitions. They were defeated on many occasions — by Haider Ali and Tipu, by the Marathas, by the Sikhs and by the Gurkhas. A little less of good fortune and they might have lost their foothold in India, or at the most, held on to certain coastal territories only.

And yet a closer scrutiny reveals, in the circumstances then existing, a certain inevitability in what happened. Good fortune there certainly was, but there must be an ability to profit by good fortune. India was then in a fluid and disorganized state, following the breakup of the Moghul empire; for many centuries it had not been so weak and helpless. Organized power having broken down, the field was left open to adventurers and new claimants for dominion. Among these adventurers and claimants, the British, and the British alone at the time, possessed many of the qualities necessary for success. Their major disadvantage was that they were foreigners coming from a far country. Yet that very disadvantage worked in their favor, for no one took them very seriously or considered them as possible contestants for the sovereignty of India. . . .

If the Marathas (and much more so the other Indian powers) were amateurish and adventurist in their methods, the British in India were thoroughly professional. Many of the British leaders were adventurous enough, but they were in no way adventurist in their policy, for which they all worked in their separate spheres. "The East India Company's Secretariat," writes Edward Thompson, "was served in the courts of Native India by a succession and galaxy of men such as even the British empire has hardly ever possessed together at any other time." One of the chief duties of the British residents at these courts was to bribe and corrupt the ministers and other officials. Their spy system was perfect, says a historian. They had complete information of the courts and armies of their adversaries, while those adversaries lived in ignorance of what the British were doing or were going to do. The fifth column of the British functioned continuously, and in moments of crisis and in the heat of war there would be defections in their favor which made a great difference. They won most of their battles before the actual fighting took place. That had been so at Plassey, and that was repeated again and again right up to the Sikh wars. A notable instance of desertion was that of a high officer in the service of Scindhia of Gwalior, who had secretly come to terms with the British and went over to them with his entire array at the moment of battle. He was re-

warded for this later by being made the ruler of a new Indian state carved out of the territories of Scindhia whom he had betrayed. That state still exists, but the man's name became a byword for treason and treachery, just as Quisling's in recent years.

The British thus represented a higher political and military organization, well knit together and having very able leaders. They were far better informed than their adversaries, and they took full advantage of the disunity and rivalries of the Indian powers. Their command of the seas gave them safe bases and opportunities to add to their resources. Even when temporarily defeated, they could recuperate and assume the offensive again. Their possession of Bengal after Plassey gave them enormous wealth and resources to carry on their warfare with the Marathas and others, and each fresh conquest added to their resources. For the Indian powers, defeat often meant a disaster which could not be remedied. . . .

We are often reminded, lest we forget, that the British rescued India from chaos and anarchy. That is true in so far as they established orderly government after this period, which the Marathas have called "the time of terror." But that chaos and anarchy were partly, at least, due to the policy of the East India Company and their representatives in India. It is also conceivable that even without the good offices of the British, so eagerly given, peace and orderly government might have been established in India after the conclusion of the struggle for supremacy. Such developments had been known to have taken place in India, as in other countries, in the course of her five thousand years of history. . . .

What was the economic background of India when all these far-reaching political changes were taking place? V. Anstey has written that right up to the eighteenth century "Indian methods of production and of industrial and commercial organization could stand comparison with those in vogue in any other part of the world." India was a highly developed manufacturing country exporting her manufactured products to Europe and other countries. Her banking system was efficient and well organized throughout the country, and the hundis or bills of exchange issued by the great business or financial houses were honored everywhere in India, as well as in Iran, and Kabul and Herat and Tashkent and other places in central Asia. Merchant capital had evolved, and there was an elaborate network of agents, jobbers, brokers, and middlemen. The shipbuilding industry was flourishing; one of the flagships of an English admiral during the Napoleonic wars had been built by an Indian firm in India. India was, in fact, as advanced industrially, commercially, and financially as any country prior to the Industrial Revolution. No such development could have taken place unless the country had enjoyed long periods of stable and peaceful government and the highways were safe for traffic and trade.

Foreign adventurers originally came to India because of the excellence of her manufactures, which had a big market in Europe. The chief business of the British East India Company in its early days was to trade with Indian goods in Europe, and very profitable trading it was, yielding enormous dividends. So efficient and highly organized were Indian methods of production, and such was the skill of India's artisans and craftsmen, that they could compete successfully even with the higher techniques of production which were being established in England. When the big machine age began in England, Indian goods continued to pour in and had to be stopped by very heavy duties, and in some cases by outright prohibition.

Clive described Murshidabad in Bengal in 1757, the very year of Plassey, as a city "as extensive, populous, and rich as the city of London, with this difference that there are individuals in the first possessing infinitely greater property than in the last." The city of Dacca in eastern Bengal was famous for its fine muslins. These two cities, important as they were, were near the periphery of Hindustan. All over the vast land there were greater cities and large numbers of big manufacturing and trading centers, and a very rapid and ingenious system of communicating news and market prices had been evolved. The great business houses often received news, even of the wars that were going on, long before dispatches reached the officials of the East India Company. The economy of India had thus advanced to as high a stage as it could reach prior to the Industrial Revolution. Whether it had the seeds of further progress in it or was too much bound up with the rigid social structure, it is difficult to say. It seems quite possible, however, that under normal conditions it would have undergone that change and begun to adapt itself, in its own way, to the new industrial conditions. And yet, though it was ripe for a change, that change itself required a revolution within its own framework. Perhaps some catalytic agent was necessary to bring about that change. It is clear that howsoever highly organized and developed its preindustrial economy was, it could not compete for long with the products of industrialized countries. It had to industrialize itself or submit to foreign economic penetration, which would have led to political interferences. As it happened, foreign political domination came first and this led to a rapid destruction of the economy she had built up, without anything positive or constructive taking its place. The East India Company represented both British political power and British vested interests and economic power. It was supreme, and being a company of merchants, it was intent on making money. Just when it was making money with amazing rapidity and in fantastic quantities, Adam Smith wrote about it in *The Wealth of Nations* in 1776: "The government of an exclusive company of merchants is perhaps the worst of all governments for any country whatever."

Though the Indian merchant and manufacturing classes were rich and spread out all over the country, and even controlled the economic structure, they had no political power. Government was despotic and still largely feudal. In fact, it was probably more feudal than it had been at some previous stages of Indian history. Hence there was no middle class strong enough to seize power, or even consciously of thinking of doing so, as in some Western countries. The people generally had grown apathetic and servile. There was thus a gap which had to be filled before any revolutionary change could take place. Perhaps this gap had been produced by the static nature of Indian society which refused to change in a changing world, for every civilization which resists change declines. That society, as constituted, had no more creative part to play. A change was overdue.

The British, at that time, were politically much more advanced. They had had their political revolution and had established the power of Parliament over that of the king. Their middle classes, conscious of their new power, were full of the impulse to expand. That vitality and energy, proof of a growing and progressive society, are indeed very evident in England. They show themselves in many ways, and most of all in the inventions and discoveries which heralded the Industrial Revolution.

*   *   *

The British have been in the city of Madras a little over 300 years; they have ruled Bengal, Bihar, etc. for almost 200 years; they extended their domination over the south roughly 150 years ago; they established themselves in the United Provinces (as they are now called), central and western India about 125 years ago; and they spread to the Punjab not quite 100 years ago. . . .

A significant fact which stands out is that those parts of India which have been longest under British rule are the poorest today. Indeed some kind of chart might be drawn up to indicate the close connection between length of British rule and progressive growth of poverty. A few large cities and some new industrial areas do not make any essential difference to this survey. What is noteworthy is the condition of the masses as a whole, and there can be no doubt that the poorest parts of India are Bengal, Bihar, Orissa and parts of the Madras presidency; the mass level and standards of living are highest in the Punjab. Bengal certainly was a very rich and prosperous province before the British came. There may be many reasons for these contrasts and differences. But it is difficult to get over the fact that Bengal, once so rich and flourishing, after 187 years of British rule, accompanied, as we are told, by strenuous attempts on the part of the British to improve its condition and to teach its people the art of self-government, is today a miserable mass of poverty-stricken, starving and dying people.

Bengal had the first full experience of British rule in India. That rule began with outright plunder, and a land revenue system which extracted the uttermost farthing not only from the living but also the dead cultivators. The English historians of India, Edward Thompson and G. T. Garrett, tell us that "a gold-lust unequalled since the hysteria that took hold of the Spaniards of Cortes' and Pizzaro's age filled the English mind. Bengal in particular was not to know peace again until she had been bled white. . . . For the monstrous financial immorality of the English conduct in India for many a year after this, Clive was largely responsible" — Clive, the great empire builder, whose statue faces the India Office in London today. It was pure loot. The "Pagoda tree" was shaken again and again till the most terrible famines ravaged Bengal. This process was called trade later on, but that made little difference. Government was this so-called trade, and trade was plunder. There are few instances in history of anything like it. And it must be remembered that this lasted, under various names and under different forms, not for a few years but for generations. The outright plunder gradually took the shape of legalized exploitation which, though not so obvious, was in reality worse. The corruption, venality, nepotism, violence, and greed of money of these early generations of British rule in India is something which passes comprehension. It is significant that one of the Hindustani words which has become part of the English language is "loot." Says Edward Thompson, and this does not refer to Bengal only, "one remembers the early history of British India which is perhaps the world's high watermark of graft."

The result of all this, even in its early stages, was the famine of 1770 which swept away over a third of the population of Bengal and Bihar. But it was all in the cause of progress, and Bengal can take pride in the fact that she helped greatly in giving birth to the Industrial Revolution in England. The American writer Brook[s] Adams tells us exactly how this happened: "The influx of Indian treasure, by adding considerably to the nation's cash capital, not only increased its stock of energy, but added much to its flexibility and the rapidity of its movement. Very soon after Plassey, the Bengal plunder began to arrive in London, and the effect appears to have been instantaneous, for all authorities agree that the 'industrial revolution' began with the year 1770. . . . Plassey was fought in 1757, and probably nothing has ever equalled the rapidity of the change that followed. In 1760 the flying shuttle appeared, and coal began to replace wood in smelting. In 1764 Hargreaves invented the spinning jenny, in 1776 Crompton contrived the mule, in 1785 Cartwright patented the power loom, and in 1768 Watt matured the steam engine. . . . But, though these machines served as outlets for the accelerating movements of the time, they did not cause the acceleration. In themselves inventions are passive, . . . waiting for a sufficient store of force to have accumulated to set them working. That store must always take the shape of money, and money not hoarded but in motion. Before the influx of the Indian treasure, and the expansion of credit which followed, no force sufficient for this purpose existed. . . . Possibly since the world began, no investment has ever yielded the profit reaped from the Indian plunder, because for nearly fifty years Great Britain stood without a competitor."[1]

The chief business of the East India Company in its early period, the very object for which it was started, was to carry Indian manufactured goods — textiles, etc., as well as spices and the like — from the East to Europe, where there was a great demand for these articles. With the developments in industrial techniques in England a new class of industrial capitalists rose there demanding a change in this policy. The British market was to be closed to Indian products and the Indian market opened to British manufactures. The British parliament, influenced by this new class, began to take a greater interest in India and the working of the East India Company. To begin with, Indian goods were excluded from Britain by legislation, and as the company held a monopoly in the Indian export business, this exclusion influenced other foreign markets also. This was followed by vigorous attempts to restrict and crush Indian manufactures by various measures and internal duties which prevented the flow of Indian goods within the country itself. British goods meanwhile had free entry. The Indian textile industry collapsed, affecting vast numbers of weavers and artisans. The process was rapid in Bengal and Bihar; elsewhere it spread gradually with the expansion of British rule and the building of railways. It continued throughout the nineteenth century, breaking up other old industries also, shipbuilding, metalwork, glass, paper, and many crafts.

To some extent this was inevitable as the older manufacturing came into conflict with the new industrial technique. But it was hastened by political and economic pressure, and no attempt was made to apply the new techniques to India. Indeed every attempt was made to prevent this happen-

[1] Brook[s] Adams, *The Law of Civilization and Decay* (1928 [originally published in 1895 — Ed.]), pp. 259–60, quoted by Kate Mitchell, *India* (1943).

ing, and thus the growth of the new industry prevented. Machinery could not be imported into India. A vacuum was created in India which could only be filled by British goods, and which also led to rapidly increasing unemployment and poverty. The classic type of modern colonial economy was built up, India becoming an agricultural colony of industrial England, supplying raw materials and providing markets for England's industrial goods.

The liquidation of the artisan class led to unemployment on a prodigious scale. What were all these scores of millions, who had so far been engaged in industry and manufacture, to do now? Where were they to go? Their old profession was no longer open to them; the way to a new one was barred. They could die of course; that way of escape from an intolerable situation is always open. They did die in tens of millions. The English governor-general of India, Lord Bentinck, reported in 1834 that "the misery hardly finds a parallel in the history of commerce. The bones of the cotton-weavers are bleaching the plains of India."

But still vast numbers of them remained, and these increased from year to year as British policy affected remoter areas of the country and created more unemployment. All these hordes of artisans and craftsmen had no jobs, no work, and all their ancient skill was useless. They drifted to the land, for the land was still there. But the land was fully occupied and could not possibly absorb them profitably. So they became a burden on the land and the burden grew, and with it grew the poverty of the country, and the standard of living fell to incredibly low levels. This compulsory back-to-the-land movement of artisans and craftsmen led to an ever-growing disproportion between agriculture and industry; agriculture became more and more the sole business of the people because of the lack of occupations and wealth-producing activities.

India became progressively ruralized. In every progressive country there has been, during the past century, a shift of population from agriculture to industry; from village to town; in India this process was reversed, as a result of British policy. The figures are instructive and significant. In the middle of the nineteenth century about 55 per cent of the population is said to have been dependent on agriculture; recently this proportion was estimated to be 74 per cent. This is a prewar figure. Though there has been greater industrial employment during the war, those dependent on agriculture actually went up in the census of 1941, owing to increase of population. The growth of a few large cities (chiefly at the expense of the smaller towns) is apt to mislead the superficial observer and give him a false idea of Indian conditions.

This, then, is the real, the fundamental cause of the appalling poverty of the Indian people, and it is of comparatively recent origin. Other causes that contribute to it are themselves the result of this poverty and chronic starvation and undernourishment — like diseases and illiteracy. Excessive population is unfortunate and steps should be taken to curb it wherever necessary; but the density in India still compares favorably with that of many industrialized countries. It is only excessive for a predominantly agricultural community, and under a proper economic system the entire population can be made productive and should add to the wealth of the country. As a matter of fact, great density of population exists only in special areas, like Bengal and the Gangetic valley, and vast areas are still sparsely populated. It is worth remembering that Great Britain is more than twice as densely populated as India.

The crisis in industry spread rapidly to the land and became a permanent crisis in agriculture. Holdings became smaller and smaller, and fragmentation proceeded to an absurd and fantastic degree. The burden of agricultural debt grew, and ownership of the land often passed to moneylenders. The number of landless laborers increased by the million. India was under an industrial-capitalist regime, but her economy was largely that of the precapitalist period,

minus many of the wealth-producing elements of that precapitalist economy. She
became a passive agent of modern industrial capitalism, suffering all its ills and with
hardly any of its advantages.

The transition from a preindustrialist
economy to an economy of capitalist industrialism involves great hardship and heavy
cost in human suffering borne by masses of
people. This was especially so in the early
days when no efforts were made to plan
such a transition or to lessen its evil results
and everything was left to individual initiative. There was this hardship in England
during this period of transition, but taken
as a whole, it was not great, as the changeover was rapid and the unemployment
caused was soon absorbed by the new industries. But that did not mean that the
cost in human suffering was not paid. It
was indeed paid, and paid in full by others,
particularly by the people of India, both by
famine and death and vast unemployment.
It may be said that a great part of the costs
of transition to industrialism in western
Europe were paid for by India, China, and
the other colonial countries whose economy
was dominated by the European powers.

It is obvious that there has been all along
abundant material for industrial development — managerial and technical ability,
skilled workers, even some capital in spite
of the continuous drain from India. The
historian Montgomery Martin, giving evidence before a committee of the British
parliament in 1840, said: "India is as much
a manufacturing country as an agricultur-
ist; and he who would seek to reduce her
to the position of an agricultural country,
seeks to lower her in the scale of civilization." That is exactly what the British in
India sought to do, continuously and persistently, and the measure of their success
is the present condition of India, after they
have held despotic sway here for a century
and a half. . . .

The world market that the new capitalism was building up would have, in any
event, affected India's economic system.
The self-sufficient village community, with

its traditional division of labor, could not
have continued in its old form. But the
change that took place was not a normal
development, and it disintegrated the whole
economic and structural basis of Indian
society. A system which had social sanc-
tions and controls behind it and was a part
of the people's cultural heritage was suddenly and forcibly changed, and another
system, administered from outside the
group, was imposed. India did not come
into a world market but became a colonial
and agricultural appendage of the British
structure.

The village community, which had so
far been the basis of Indian economy, was
disintegrated, losing both its economic and
administrative functions. In 1830 Sir
Charles Metcalfe, one of the ablest of British officials in India, described these communities in words which have often been
quoted: "The village communities are little
republics having nearly everything they
want within themselves; and almost independent of foreign relations. They seem to
last where nothing else lasts. This union
of the village communities, each one forming a separate little State in itself . . . is in
a high degree conducive to their happiness,
and to the enjoyment of a great portion of
freedom and independence."

The destruction of village industries was
a powerful blow to these communities. The
balance between industry and agriculture
was upset, the traditional division of labor
was broken up, and numerous stray individuals could not be easily fitted into any
group activity. A more direct blow came
from the introduction of the landlord system, changing the whole conception of
ownership of land. This conception had
been one of communal ownership, not so
much of the land as of the produce of the
land. Possibly not fully appreciating this,
but more probably taking the step deliberately for reasons of their own, the British
governors, themselves representing the English landlord class, introduced something
resembling the English system in India. At
first they appointed revenue-farmers for

short terms, that is persons who were made responsible for the collection of the revenue or land tax and payment of it to the Government. Later these revenue-farmers developed into landlords. The village community was deprived of all control over the land and its produce; what had always been considered as the chief interest and concern of that community now became the private property of the newly created landowner. This led to the breakdown of the joint life and corporate character of the community, and the cooperative system of services and functions began to disappear gradually.

The introduction of this type of property in land was not only a great economic change, but it went deeper and struck at the whole Indian conception of a cooperative group social structure. A new class, the owners of land, appeared; a class created by, and therefore to a large extent identified with, the British government. The breakup of the old system created new problems, and probably the beginnings of the new Hindu-Moslem problem can be traced to it. The landlord system was first introduced in Bengal and Bihar, where big landowners were created under the system known as the Permanent Settlement. It was later realized that this was not advantageous to the state, as the land revenue had been fixed and could not be enhanced. Fresh settlements in other parts of India were therefore made for a period only, and enhancements in revenue took place from time to time. In some provinces a kind of peasant proprietorship was established. The extreme rigor applied to the collection of revenue resulted, especially in Bengal, in the ruin of the old landed gentry, and new people from the monied and business classes took their place. Thus Bengal became a province predominantly of Hindu landlords, while their tenants, though both Hindu and Moslem, were chiefly the latter.

Big landowners were created by the British after their own English pattern, chiefly because it was far easier to deal with a few individuals than with a vast peasantry. The objective was to collect as much money in the shape of revenue and as speedily as possible. If an owner failed at the stipulated time, he was immediately pushed out and another took his place. It was also considered necessary to create a class whose interests were identified with the British. The fear of revolt filled the minds of British officials in India, and they referred to this repeatedly in their papers. Governor-General Lord William Bentinck said in 1829: "If security was wanting against extensive popular tumult or revolution, I should say that the Permanent Settlement, though a failure in many other respects, has this great advantage at least, of having created a vast body of rich landed proprietors deeply interested in the continuance of British Dominion and having complete command over the mass of the people."

British rule thus consolidated itself by creating new classes and vested interests who were tied up with that rule and whose privileges depended on its continuance. There were the landowners and the princes, and there were a large number of subordinate members of the services in various departments of government, from the patwari, the village headman, upward. The two essential branches of government were the revenue system and the police. At the head of both of these in each district was the collector or district magistrate who was the linchpin of the administration. He functioned as an autocrat in his district, combining in himself executive, judicial, revenue, and police functions. If there were any small Indian states adjoining the area under his control, he was also the British agent for them.

Then there was the Indian Army, consisting of British and Indian troops but officered entirely by Englishmen. This was reorganized repeatedly, especially after the Mutiny of 1857, and ultimately became organizationally linked up with the British Army. This was so arranged as to balance its different elements and keep the British troops in key positions. "Next to the grand counterpoise of a sufficient European force, comes the counterpoise of natives against natives," says the official report on reorganization in 1858. The primary function of these forces was to serve as an army of occupation — "Internal Security Troops" they were called, and a majority of these were British. The Frontier Province served as a training ground for the British Army at India's expense. The field army (chiefly Indian) was meant for service abroad and it took part in numerous British imperial wars and expeditions, India always bearing the cost. Steps were taken to segregate Indian troops from the rest of the population.

Thus India had to bear the cost of her own conquest, and then of her transfer (or sale) from the East India Company to the British crown, and for the extension of the British empire to Burma and elsewhere, and expeditions to Africa, Persia, etc., and for her defense against Indians themselves. She was not only used as a base for imperial purposes, without any reimbursement for this, but she had further to pay for the training of part of the British Army in England — "capitation" charges these were called. Indeed India was charged for all manner of other expenses incurred by Britain, such as the maintenance of British diplomatic and consular establishments in China and Persia, the entire cost of the telegraph line from England to India, part of the expenses of the British Mediterranean fleet, and even the receptions given to the sultan of Turkey in London.

The building of railways in India, undoubtedly desirable and necessary, was done in an enormously wasteful way. The government of India guaranteed 5 per cent interest on all capital invested, and there was no need to check or estimate what was necessary. All purchases were made in England.

The civil establishment of government was also run on a lavish and extravagant scale, all the highly paid positions being reserved for Europeans. The process of indianization of the administrative machine was very slow and only became noticeable in the twentieth century. This process, far

from transferring any power to Indian hands, proved yet another method of strengthening British rule. The really key positions remained in British hands, and Indians in the administration could only function as the agents of British rule.

To all these methods must be added the deliberate policy, pursued throughout the period of British rule, of creating divisions among Indians, of encouraging one group at the cost of the other. This policy was openly admitted in the early days of their rule, and indeed it was a natural one for an imperial power. With the growth of the nationalist movement, that policy took subtler and more dangerous forms, and though denied, functioned more intensively than ever.

Nearly all our major problems today have grown up during British rule and as a direct result of British policy: the princes; the minority problem; various vested interests, foreign and Indian; the lack of industry and the neglect of agriculture; the extreme backwardness in the social services; and, above all, the tragic poverty of the people. . . .

The modern type of finance imperialism added new kinds of economic exploitation which were unknown in earlier ages. The record of British rule in India during the nineteenth century must necessarily depress and anger an Indian, and yet it illustrates the superiority of the British in many fields, not least in their capacity to profit by our disunity and weaknesses. A people who are weak and who are left behind in the march of time invite trouble and ultimately have only themselves to blame. If British imperialism with all its consequences was, in the circumstances, to be expected in the natural order of events, so also was the growth of opposition to it inevitable, and the final crisis between the two.

*   *   *

One remarkable contradiction meets us at every turn in considering the record of British rule in India. The British became dominant in India, and the foremost power in the world, because they were the heralds of the new big-machine industrial civilization. They represented a new historic force which was going to change the world, and were thus, unknown to themselves, the forerunners and representatives of change and revolution. And yet they deliberately tried to prevent change, except in so far as this was necessary to consolidate their position and help them in exploiting the country and its people to their own advantage. Their outlook and objectives were reactionary, partly because of the background of the social class that came here, but chiefly because of a deliberate desire to check changes in a progressive direction as these might strengthen the Indian people and thus ultimately weaken the British hold on India. The fear of the people runs through all their thought and policy, for they did not want to and could not merge with them, and were destined to remain an isolated foreign ruling group surrounded by an entirely different and hostile humanity. Changes, and some changes in a progressive direction, did come, but they came in spite of British policy, although the impetus for that change was the impact of the new West through the British.

Individual Englishmen, educationalists, Orientalists, journalists, missionaries, and others, played an important part in bringing Western culture to India, and in their attempts to do so often came into conflict with their own government. That government feared the effects of the spread of modern education and put many obstacles in its way, and yet it was due to the pioneering efforts of able and earnest Englishmen, who gathered enthusiastic groups of Indian students around them, that English thought and literature and political tradition were introduced to India. . . . Even the British government, in spite of its dislike of education, was compelled by circumstances to arrange for the training of clerks for its growing establishment. It could not afford to bring out from England large numbers of people to serve in this subordinate capacity. So education grew slowly,

and though it was a limited and perverted education, it opened the doors and windows of the mind to new ideas and dynamic thoughts. . . .

While private printing presses were not encouraged, government could not carry on its work without printing, and official presses were therefore started in Calcutta and Madras and elsewhere. The first private printing press was started by the Baptist missionaries in Serampore, and the first newspaper was started by an Englishman in Calcutta in 1780.

All these and other like changes crept in, gradually influencing the Indian mind and giving rise to the "modern" consciousness. Only a small group was directly influenced by the thought of Europe, for India clung to her own philosophic background, considering it superior to that of the West. The real impact and influence of the West were on the practical side of life, which was obviously superior to the Eastern. The new techniques — the railway train, the printing press, other machinery, more efficient ways of warfare — could not be ignored, and these came up against old methods of thought almost unawares, by indirect approaches, creating a conflict in the mind of India. The most obvious and far-reaching change was the breakup of the agrarian system and the introduction of conceptions of private property and landlordism. Money economy had crept in, and "land became a marketable commodity. What had once been held rigid by custom was dissolved by money."

* * *

The impact of Western culture on India was the impact of a dynamic society, of a "modern" consciousness, on a static society wedded to medieval habits of thought, which, however sophisticated and advanced in its own way, could not progress because of its inherent limitations. And yet, curiously enough, the agents of this historic process were not only wholly unconscious of their mission in India but, as a class, actually represented no such process. In England their class fought this historic process, but the forces opposed to them were too strong for them and could not be held back. In India they had a free field and were successful in applying the brakes to that very change and progress which, in the larger context, they represented. They encouraged and consolidated the position of the socially reactionary groups in India, and opposed all those who worked for political and social change. If change came, it was in spite of them or as an incidental and unexpected consequence of their other activities. The introduction of the steam engine and the railway was a big step toward a change of the medieval structure, but it was intended to consolidate their rule and facilitate the exploitation, for their own benefit, of the interior of the country. This contradiction between the deliberate policy of the British authorities in India and some of its unintended consequences produces a certain confusion and masks that policy itself. Change came to India because of this impact of the West, but it came almost in spite of the British in India. They succeeded in slowing down the pace of that change to such an extent that even today the transition is very far from complete.

The feudal landlords and their kind who came from England to rule over India had the landlord's view of the world. To them India was a vast estate belonging to the East India Company, and the landlord was the best and the natural representative of his estate and his tenants. That view continued even after the East India Company handed over its estate of India to the British crown, being paid very handsome compensation at India's cost. (Thus began the public debt of India. It was India's purchase money, paid by India.) The British government of India then became the landlords (or landlords' agents). For all practical purposes they considered themselves "India," just as the Duke of Devonshire might be considered "Devonshire" by his peers. The millions of people who lived and functioned in India were just some kind of landlord's tenants who had to pay their rents and cesses and to keep their

place in the natural feudal order. For them a challenge to that order was an offense against the very moral basis of the universe and a denial of a divine dispensation.

This somewhat metaphysical conception of British rule in India has not changed fundamentally, though it is expressed differently now. The old method of obvious rack-renting gave place to more subtle and devious devices. It was admitted that the landlord should be benevolent toward his tenantry and should seek to advance their interests. It was even agreed that some of the more loyal and faithful among the tenants should be promoted to the estate office and share in a subordinate way in the administration. But no challenge to the system of landlordism could be tolerated. The estate must continue to function as it used to, even when it changed hands. When pressure of events made some change inevitable, it was stipulated that all the faithful employees in the estate office should continue, all the old and new friends, followers and dependents of the landlord should be provided for, the old pensioners should continue to draw their pensions, the old landlord himself should now function as a benevolent patron and adviser of the estate, and thus all attempts to bring about essential changes should be frustrated.

*   *   *

Though the revolt [of 1857–58] had directly affected only certain parts of the country, it had shaken up the whole of India, and particularly the British administration. The government set about reorganizing their entire system; the British crown, that is the parliament, took over the country from the East India Company; the Indian Army, which had begun the revolt by its mutiny, was organized afresh. The techniques of British rule, which had already been well established, were now clarified and confirmed and deliberately acted upon. Essentially these were: the creation and protection of vested interests bound up with British rule; and a policy of balancing and counterpoise of different elements, and the encouragement of fissiparous tendencies and division among them.

The princes and the big landlords were the basic vested interests thus created and encouraged. But now a new class, even more tied up with British rule, grew in importance. This consisted of the Indian members of the services, usually in subordinate positions. Previously the employment of Indians had been avoided except when this could not be helped, and Munro had pleaded for such employment. Experience had now demonstrated that Indians so employed were so dependent on the British administration and rule that they could be relied upon and treated as agents of that rule. . . .

Thus began the process of the indianization of the administrative machine in its subordinate ranks, all real power and initiative being, however, concentrated in the hands of the English personnel. . . . This indianization became the most effective method of strengthening British rule. It created a civil army and garrison everywhere, which was more important even than the military army of occupation. There were some members of this civil army who were able and patriotic and nationalistically inclined; but like the soldier, who also may be patriotic in his individual capacity, they were bound up by the army code and discipline, and the price of disobedience, desertion, and revolt was heavy. Not only was this civil army created, but the hope and prospect of employment in it affected and demoralized a vast and growing number of others. There was a measure of prestige and security in it and a pension at the end of the term of service, and if a sufficient subservience was shown to one's superior officers, other failings did not count. These civil employees were the intermediaries between the British authorities and the people, and if they had to be obsequious to their superiors, they could be arrogant and exact obedience from their own inferiors and the people at large.

The lack of other avenues of employment, other ways of making a living, added additional importance to government service. A few could become lawyers or doctors, but even so, success was by no means assured. Industry hardly existed. Trade was largely in the hands of certain hereditary classes who had a peculiar aptitude for it and who helped each other. The new education did not fit any one for trade or industry; its chief aim was government service. Education was so limited as to offer few openings for a professional career; other social services were almost nonexistent. So government service remained and, as the colleges poured out their graduates, even the growing government services could not absorb them all, and a fierce competition arose. The unemployed graduates and others formed a pool from which government could always draw; they were a potential threat to the security of even the employed. Thus the British government in India became not only the biggest employer, but for all practical purposes the sole big employer (including railways), and a vast bureaucratic machine was built up, strictly managed and controlled at the top. This enormous patronage was exercised to strengthen the British hold on the country, to crush discordant and disagreeable elements, and to promote rivalry and discord among various groups anxiously looking forward to employment in government service. It led to demoralization and conflict, and the government could play one group against the other. . . .

Again we notice in India that inherent contradiction in British rule. Having brought about the political unification of the country and thus let loose new dynamic forces which thought not only in terms of that unity but aimed at the freedom of India, the British government tried to disrupt that very unity it had helped to create. That disruption was not thought of in political terms then as a splitting up of India; it was aimed at the weakening of nationalist elements so that British rule might continue over the whole country. But it was nonetheless an attempt at disruption, by giving greater importance to the Indian states than they had ever had before, by encouraging reactionary elements and looking to them for support, by promoting divisions and encouraging one group against another, by encouraging fissiparous tendencies due to religion or province, and by organizing Quisling classes which were afraid of a change which might engulf them. All this was a natural and understandable policy for a foreign imperialist power to pursue, and it is a little naive to be surprised at it, harmful from the Indian nationalist point of view though it was. But the fact that it was so must be remembered if we are to understand subsequent developments. Out of this policy arose those "important elements in India's national life" of which we are reminded so often today; which were created and encouraged to disagree and disrupt, and are now called upon to agree among themselves.

Because of this natural alliance of the British power with the reactionaries in India, it became the guardian and upholder of many an evil custom and practice which it otherwise condemned. India was custom-ridden when the British came, and the tyranny of old custom is often a terrible thing. Yet customs change and are forced to adapt themselves to some extent to a changing environment. Hindu law was largely custom, and as custom changed, the law also was applied in a different way. Indeed there was no provision of Hindu law which could not be changed by custom. The British replaced this elastic customary law by judicial decisions based on the old texts, and these decisions became precedents which had to be rigidly followed. That was, in theory, an advantage, as it produced greater uniformity and certainty. But, in the way it was done, it resulted in the perpetuation of the ancient law unmodified by subsequent customs. Thus the old law, which in some particulars and in various places had been changed by custom and was thus out-of-date, was petrified, and every tendency to change it in the well-known customary way was suppressed. It was still open to a group to prove a custom

overriding the law, but this was extraordinarily difficult in the law courts. Change could only come by positive legislation, but the British government, which was the legislating authority, had no wish to antagonize the conservative elements on whose support it counted. When later some legislative powers were given to partially elected assemblies, every attempt to promote social reform legislation was frowned upon by the authorities and sternly discouraged.

*   *   *

A nation, like an individual, has many personalities, many approaches to life. If there is a sufficiently strong organic bond between these different personalities, it is well; otherwise those personalities split up and lead to disintegration and trouble. Normally, there is a continuous process of adjustment going on and some kind of an equilibrium is established. If normal development is arrested, or sometimes if there is some rapid change which is not easily assimilated, then conflict arises between those different personalities. In the mind and spirit of India, below the surface of our superficial conflicts and divisions, there has been this fundamental conflict due to a long period of arrested growth. A society, if it is to be both stable and progressive, must have a certain more or less fixed foundation of principles as well as a dynamic outlook. Both appear to be necessary. Without the dynamic outlook there is stagnation and decay; without some fixed basis of principle there is likely to be disintegration and destruction.

In India from the earliest days there was a search for those basic principles, for the unchanging, the universal, the absolute. Yet the dynamic outlook was also present and an appreciation of life and the changing world. On these foundations a stable and progressive society was built up, though the stress was always more on stability and security and the survival of the race. In later years the dynamic aspect began to fade away, and in the name of eternal principles the social structure was made rigid and unchanging. It was, as a matter of fact, not wholly rigid, and it did change gradually and continuously. But the ideology behind it and the general framework continued unchanged. . . .

The very thing India lacked, the modern West possessed and possessed to excess. It had the dynamic outlook. It was engrossed in the changing world, caring little for ultimate principles, the unchanging, the universal. It paid little attention to duties and obligations, and emphasized rights. It was active, aggressive, acquisitive, seeking power and domination, living in the present and ignoring the future consequences of its actions. Because it was dynamic, it was progressive and full of life, but that life was a fevered one and the temperature kept on rising progressively.

If Indian civilization went to seed because it became static, self-absorbed, and inclined to narcissism, the civilization of the Modern West, with all its great and manifold achievements, does not appear to have been a conspicuous success or to have thus far solved the basic problems of life. Conflict is inherent in it, and periodically it indulges in self-destruction on a colossal scale. It seems to lack something to give it stability, some basic principles to give meaning to life, though what these are I cannot say. Yet because it is dynamic and full of life and curiosity, there is hope for it.

India, as well as China, must learn from the West, for the modern West has much to teach, and the spirit of the age is represented by the West. But the West is also obviously in need of learning much, and its advances in technology will bring it little comfort if it does not learn some of the deeper lessons of life, which have absorbed the minds of thinkers in all ages and in all countries.

India had become static, and yet it would be utterly wrong to imagine that she was unchanging. No change at all means death. Her very survival as a highly evolved nation shows that there was some process of continuous adaptation going on. When the British came to India, though technologically somewhat backward she was still among the advanced commercial nations of the world. Technical changes would undoubtedly have come and changed India as they had changed some Western countries. But her normal development was arrested by the British power. Industrial growth was checked, and as a consequence social growth was also arrested. The normal power relationships of society could not adjust themselves and find an equilibrium, as all power was concentrated in the alien authority, which based itself on force and encouraged groups and classes which had ceased to have any real significance. Indian life thus progressively became more artificial, for many of the individuals and groups who seemed to play an important rôle in it had no vital functions left and were there only because of the importance given to them by the alien power. They had long ago finished their rôle in history and would have been pushed aside by new forces if they had not been given foreign protection. They became straw-stuffed symbols or protégés of foreign authority, thereby cutting themselves further away from the living currents of the nation. Normally they would have been weeded out or diverted to some more appropriate function by revolution or democratic process. But so long as foreign authoritarian rule continued, no such development could take place. And so India was cluttered up with these emblems of the past and the real changes that were taking place were hidden behind an artificial façade. No true social balances or power relationships within society could develop or become evident, and unreal problems assumed an undue importance.

Most of our problems today are due to this arrested growth and the prevention by British authority of normal adjustments taking place. The problem of the Indian princes is easily capable of solution if the external factor is removed. The minorities problem is utterly unlike any minority problem elsewhere; indeed it is not a minority problem at all. There are many aspects of it, and no doubt we are to blame for it in the past and in the present. And yet, at the back of these and other problems is the desire of the British government to preserve, as far as possible, the existing economy and political organization of the Indian people, and, for this purpose, to encourage and preserve the socially backward groups in their present condition. Political and economic progress has not only been directly prevented, but also made dependent on the agreement of reactionary groups and vested interests, and this may be purchased only by confirming them in their privileged positions or giving them a dominating voice in any future arrangement, and thus putting formidable obstacles in the way of real change and progress.

* * *

The independence of the United States of America is more or less contemporaneous with the loss of freedom by India. Surveying the past century and a half, an Indian looks somewhat wistfully and longingly at the vast progress made by the United States during this period and compares it with what has been done and what has not been done in his own country. It is true no doubt that the Americans have many virtues and we have many failings, that America offered a virgin field and almost a clean slate to write upon while we were cluttered up with ancient memories and traditions. And yet perhaps it is not inconceivable that if Britain had not undertaken this great burden in India and, as she tells us, endeavored for so long to teach us the difficult art of self-government, of which we had been so ignorant, India might not only have been freer and more prosperous but also far more advanced in science and art and all that makes life worth living.

Re-statement and Balance Sheet

SIR REGINALD COUPLAND

Sir Reginald Coupland (1884–1952) was Beit Professor of Colonial History at Oxford University from 1920 to 1948. His many published works include *Wilberforce, a Narrative* (1923), *The American Revolution and the British Empire* (1930), *The British Anti-Slavery Movement* (1933), *East Africa and Its Invaders* (1938), and *Raffles of Singapore* (1946). In *India: A Re-statement* (1945) he sought to summarize the record of British rule in India, at a time when it was clear that that rule would soon be coming to an end.

THE POLITICAL ASPECT

1. *The Intervention of Parliament.* That the [British] Raj made a discreditable start is not in question. The black facts of the decade or so after Plassey are well known — the misrule and misery of Bengal and the great fortunes amassed by the [East India] Company's servants, partly, as Clive protested, by openly accepting "presents" in accordance with immemorial Indian custom, partly in even more disreputable ways. Less familiar is the unsavoury scandal of the Nabob of Arcot's debts — the organised exploitation of a ruler's extravagance by a group of British sharks. The cause of all this is also not in doubt. It was the inevita-

From Sir Reginald Coupland, *India: A Re-statement* (London, 1945), pp. 42–70. By permission of J. Simmons, literary executor of Sir Reginald Coupland.

ble result, human nature being what it is, of power without responsibility. The Company's servants were the masters of Bengal and other territories, but they were not responsible for their government. Though it was they and their Indian agents rather than the puppets on the throne who were in fact obeyed, they still regarded themselves as traders only; and, since they had always been tacitly allowed to implement their nominal salaries by trading on their own account, some of them used their power to enrich themselves without any sense of the duty towards the Indian people which the possession of that power implied.

If this period of exploitation in its sinister sense was inevitable, so was its end, as soon as British public opinion became aware of what was happening in India. The disclosure was brought about mainly in two ways. First the disorganisation of Bengal, however profitable for the Company's individual servants on the spot, meant a steep fall in the dividends of its shareholders at home. Secondly, there could be no mistaking the significance of the "Nabobs," as they were called, the men who had been coming home, still in the prime of life, yet very wealthy, and proceeding to buy their way into society and even into Parliament. The reaction was threefold. There was a business reaction. It was borne in upon the "City" that bad government was fatal to good trade, and good trade was more than ever desirable in India now that the loss of the American Colonies seemed to have thrown the economic balance of the Empire over from West to East. There was a political reaction. The Company, it appeared, was creating in India an *imperium in imperio*: it was clearly time for the British Government to assert its authority over British subjects anywhere under the British flag. There was also a moral reaction. The public conscience was startled by the story of tyranny and corruption, some of it highly coloured, which had come to light. The impeachment of Warren Hastings, it is now admitted, was a clumsy and unfair method of dealing with his particular case;

but it is worth remembering that he would probably not have been tried at all if Pitt had not insisted that British conduct in India must be governed by British ideas of liberty and justice and not by Eastern custom; and, while Burke's indictment was pitifully overstrained, there was no doubting the sincerity of his moral indignation.

The outcome of this threefold reaction to events in India was a consensus of public opinion that the power which the force of circumstances had put into British hands must no longer be divorced from responsibility; that the primary British task in India was now not to trade, important though that still was, but to rule; and that that rule, which, as Burke said, was in the nature of a "trust" for the benefit of the Indian people, must be controlled by the British Government and Parliament. . . .

[By] the Act of 1784 . . . the Company's administrative system was retained as a matter of convenience, but it was firmly subjected to the British Government's "superintendence and control." The directors still appointed and instructed the officials, but the instructions could now be varied and the officials recalled by a Board of Control whose ministerial president soon came to exercise something like the powers and responsibilities of the later Secretary of State for India.

Under this so-called "dual system" the Company continued to carry on its business. It was not till 1813 that it was deprived of its monopoly of Eastern trade except with China and in tea, and not till 1833 that its commercial side was finally wound up. But after 1784 it ceased to be only or even primarily a business concern: it had become primarily an instrument of government, which, like any other instrument of British government at home or overseas, was under the ultimate control of the British Parliament and people. The twofold purpose to which that control was to be directed was defined by Pitt when he introduced the bill. It was intended, he told the House of Commons, on the one hand "to confirm and enlarge the advantages derived by this country from its connexion with India" and on the other hand "to render that connexion a blessing to the native Indians."

2. *Bureaucracy*. The government of British India by Councils of officials at the Centre and in the Provinces, confirmed by the Act of 1784, was to be modified in course of time by the intrusion of unofficial and popular elements; but this process, which will be described in the next part of this book, did not begin till 1861 and did not lead to any real transfer of legislative power till 1909 or of executive power till 1919. Till the twentieth century the British Raj was a pure and highly centralised bureaucracy, with an unbroken chain of official responsibility running from the Provinces to the Centre and from the Centre on to the British Government and Parliament. But the word "bureaucracy" may be misleading if it suggests that the officials were all working at their desks in government offices: they were mostly out in the country and out of doors. Nor, of course, did the "bureaucrats" enjoy a privileged legal status. There was no *droit administratif*. Like officials in England they were subject to the ordinary law.

The main crank of this great machine of government was the administrative corps which came to be called the Indian Civil Service. In character and purpose its members were very different from the Company's agents in the bad days after Plassey. The new regime of State control had brought with it a new sense of public duty. Practical steps were taken to make a recurrence of the old scandals impossible. Officials' pay was raised and they were forbidden under penalty to engage in private trade or accept "presents." Cadets for the service were told to regard themselves no longer as "agents of a commercial concern" but as "ministers and officers of a powerful sovereign," charged with "sacred trusts" for the good government of British India and the prosperity and happiness of its people.[1]

[1] Governor-General Wellesley's Minute in Council, 18 August 1800.

No sober critic denies that on the whole the members of the I.C.S. have been true to those trusts. It is safe, indeed, to say that no bureaucracy has ever maintained a higher standard of ability and integrity. . . . The great majority of them became District Officers, the men on each of whom lay the direct responsibility for the welfare of an area often larger than an English county and containing perhaps a million or more inhabitants. Till, in relatively recent times, the administration became more elaborate, office work increased, and new social services were established with their own personnel, the District Officer's duties were not only of almost infinite variety, they brought him into personal contact with the poor and ignorant countryfolk entrusted to his care — looking after their humble needs, listening to their grievances, settling their disputes, advising on their crops, trying to persuade them to make their villages cleaner and healthier, and so forth. He knew it was good work he was doing, and he knew, too, that the countryfolk appreciated it. "We are his children," they would say of him: "he is our *ma bap*, our mother and father." And for the fortunate who rose to the top the sense of exercising this paternal power deepened with the broadening of its scope. It was a great thing to be responsible for directing and superintending the government of a Province — a country, it might be, of forty or fifty million people.

Next in importance to the I.C.S. was the Indian Police Service. . . . Later came the new technical Services — education, agriculture, forestry, public works, and so on — but, unlike the I.C.S. and I.P. which were mainly British in personnel, they soon contained a substantial proportion of Indians. And, ranking beneath these so-called Superior or All-India Services, were the multitudinous Provincial Services staffed entirely by Indians. The growth of nationalist agitation in course of time was bound to create the impression that the great bureaucracy it assailed was composed of foreigners; and foreigners, it is true, controlled it and held most of its key positions. But of its total personnel — in 1900, for example — over 500,000 were Indian and only about 4,000 British.

The British fraction might well have been even smaller: for, from about 1820 onwards, some of the ablest and most far-sighted British officials strongly criticised the policy of keeping all the higher administrative posts — those, in fact, that were held by the members of the I.C.S. — in British hands. . . .

In the proclamation of 1858 which inaugurated the new post-Mutiny dispensation, Queen Victoria declared it to be her will

that, so far as may be, our subjects of whatever race or creed be freely and impartially admitted to offices in our service, the duties of which they may be qualified by their education, ability, and integrity duly to discharge.

To fulfill this promise in the spirit as well as the letter a more wholehearted effort was needed than the admission of Indians to the competitive examination for the I.C.S. in England (1858) or the nomination of Indians in India (1879). And that effort was not made. One Indian entered the I.C.S. in 1864, three more in 1871. As late as 1913 over 80 per cent of the highest and best-paid posts in the civil service as a whole were still in British hands.

This reluctance to associate Indians with the administration at its highest levels was not wholly due to British selfishness. There were far fewer educated Indians to choose from in the second half of the nineteenth century than there are now, and it was not unnatural that the British authorities in India should feel that the great administrative machine which they had made and in which they took a proper pride would not be run so well by Indians. There was also, at a later stage, the question of security. If the growth of a militant nationalism was from one standpoint an argument for Indianising the administration, from another it was an argument for maintaining its strength and unity.

3. *Law and Liberty*. If the bureaucracy

of the British Raj was a kind of despotism, it was a very different kind from that which the Indian people had experienced before the British came.

In the first place, the British Raj was stronger than any of its predecessors, stronger even than the Mogul Empire, and this enabled it to keep India, as never before, safe from attack without and united and at peace within. The old menace of invasion was dispelled. No hostile army crossed the frontier till 1942. The countryside was no longer swept from time to time by warring and rapacious hosts. The main highways were no longer infested by bands of brigands. Villagers could sleep of nights: their lives and property were safer now than they had ever been.

Secondly, the British Raj replaced arbitrary despotism by the rule of law. By becoming British subjects many millions of Indians acquired "a government of laws, not of men," and therewith as full a protection of their personal rights by impersonal justice and as wide a measure of civil liberty as any people in the world enjoyed. As to the content of the law, the existing laws were consolidated and codified in accordance with "the indisputable principle," as a British parliamentary committee put it, "that the interests of the Native subjects are to be consulted in preference to those of Europeans whenever the two come into competition, and that therefore the laws ought to be adapted rather to the feelings and habits of the Natives than to those of Europeans."[2] The adoption of English judicial procedure, it is sometimes argued, was unwise, since it was ill suited to the backward conditions of Indian country life. But otherwise the creation of the new courts of justice was an almost unqualified gain. They obtained, wrote an experienced Indian nationalist, "a prestige and authority unknown in Asia" outside the areas of European rule.[3] They planted in the Indian mind a new respect for law as something to

[2] *Parliamentary Papers*, 1831–2, viii. 21.
[3] S. K. Datta, *Asiatic Asia* (London, 1902), p. 129.

which even the strongest Government must bow. The value of this gift has yet to be put to its final proof; for it is on allegiance to a sovereign law that the peace and stability of the free India of the future must mainly depend.

Thirdly, the British Raj brought with it from the West certain standards of humanity which Indian society had not yet attained. Early action was taken to suppress female infanticide. After long hesitation and in the teeth of orthodox Hindu opposition, to aid and abet a performance of *suttee* was declared to be culpable homicide and, if it were involuntary, murder. The gangs of Thugs, who strangled harmless wayfarers in the service of the goddess Kali, were broken up. Human sacrifice, which had lingered on in some primitive hill districts, was stamped out. The slave trade was stifled, the legal status of slavery was abolished, and in 1860 the owning of slaves was finally prohibited.

Fourthly, while the British Raj withheld political liberty from the Indian people, it gave them civil liberty. It permitted and protected freedom of thought or opinion. In the matter of religion, in particular, all the communities, where they were in a minority as much as where they were in a majority, were free to profess their faith and to practise its rites and ceremonies.[4] Nor were they subjected to any propagandist pressure: for the Government scrupulously refrained — too scrupulously, some thought — from giving any official backing to Christian missions. With freedom of opinion went freedom to express it, in newspapers or books or on the public platform, and to form associations to expound it, with only those restrictions which, when Indian nationalism became militant and communal strife increased, seemed necessary to combat incendiary agitation. It

might, indeed, be a salutary experience for those critics who accept the "extremist" picture of the British Raj as a tyranny scarcely distinguishable from Nazism to listen to the bitter speeches or to read the outspoken articles in which Indian politicians or journalists have long been accustomed to say what they think about their Government. In stressing the want of political liberty, the value of civil liberty for the great multitude of ordinary folk is apt to be forgotten.

It may be said, lastly, that, if the British Raj was not "government by consent of the governed," it was government with their acquiescence. The proof of that lies in the fact that in a country not much smaller than Europe, with a population rising by the end of the nineteenth century towards 300 millions, there were only about 60,000 British soldiers and about 4,000 British officials. So small a "garrison" would have been an absurdity if the mass of the Indian people had felt that British rule was intolerably unjust or inhumane. That they learned to believe in its justice has already been remarked. As to its humanity, by the normal standards of Western civilization, the record speaks for itself. There is only one serious stain on it since the repression of the Mutiny — the tragedy at Amritsar in 1919. . . .

THE ECONOMIC ASPECT

1. *Economic Development.* Next to the maintenance of security and the establishment of law and order, the British Government was confronted with the huge task of providing India with the material equipment of a modern state. It was a poor country. Nine-tenths of its people were engaged in wringing a bare subsistence from the soil; there were relatively few towns; and the rural districts — so few and bad were the roads — were virtually isolated from one another and still more from the outer world. Production was mainly for local consumption. Recurrent shortages in the local rainfall meant starvation on a ghastly scale.

[4]Except such ritual practices as were inhumane or murderous, e.g., *suttee* and *thuggee*. [The Hindu practice of *suttee* was the immolation, voluntarily or by force, of a widow on the funeral pyre of her dead husband. *Thuggee* is the name given to the ritual murders which were practised by men known as *Thugs*. — Ed.]

The first immediate economic need — and it was no less required for strategic and administrative purposes — was a better system of communications. Already before the Mutiny new trunk roads and innumerable lesser roads and bridges had been built, steamship services provided on the greater rivers, ports enlarged and improved, and the construction of railways begun; and with the railways came the telegraph and a cheap and uniform postal service.

The second immediate need was irrigation — to combat drought and to improve the yield and extend the area of cultivation — and even more impressive than the spread of the network of rails and wires over India was the cutting of canals through its thirsty sun-baked soil. By 1900 India possessed far the greatest system of irrigation in the world. Before the present war more than 32 million acres of British India were watered by Government works. Large areas, especially in the dry north-west, which had been nothing but arid wilderness, were transformed into fertile crop-land, and on much of it hundreds of thousands of peasants from overcrowded districts found new homes and means of livelihood.

Railways and canals facilitated the task of grappling with famine. Besides direct measures for the relief of destitution and unemployment, it was possible now to bring surplus food in bulk from more fortunate areas. "Famine policy" became one of the major preoccupations of the Central and Provincial Governments, till the inevitably recurring periods of excessive drought no longer meant, as hitherto they had so often meant, that the population of whole districts was confronted with beggary and starvation. The catastrophe in Bengal in 1943 was a grim reminder of the fate which earlier generations had regularly undergone and of the foresight and efficiency and public spirit needed to avert it.

Meantime the country as a whole was undergoing an economic revolution. In the first place the new political unity of India, or at least of British India, was reflected in a new economic unity. Innumerable local barriers to trade were swept away, and British India — so unlike Europe — became one great area of free trade. In the second place the introduction of Western business methods, the creation of a modern banking system, the development of commercial law, together with the building of the railways and the expansion of sea transport, brought all India for the first time into the complex of world economics. The isolation of the country-side was broken down. The price of the peasant's produce rose from its poor local level to those prevailing in India as a whole and even overseas. After the opening of the Suez Canal in 1869, which reduced the length of the voyage to Europe to about one-quarter of what it had been round the Cape, Indian wheat could be sold in the world-market at a world-price. And new developments in primary production became possible and profitable. Plantations, once limited to indigo, were extended to coffee and tea. The growth of jute kept pace with its fast-growing manufacture. That the financing and management of this new enterprise were mainly British accorded with nineteenth-century notions of free trade and *laissez faire*. It was not the Government's doing. There was no such alliance between Government and commerce as has become a familiar feature of the modern world. The officials left to the "box-wallahs" a business that was no business of theirs. Even the social gulf of an earlier day in England remained unbridged. But, if British bankers and shopkeepers and planters were not assisted by the Government, they could invest their money and run their own concerns in India on the same sort of terms as in Argentina, say, or China. Naturally they retained most of the profit, which in some lines was very high, but not all of it. Salaries and wages were mainly Indian-earned: the bulk of the staff in banks and business, the whole of the labour force on the plantations, was Indian. Nor, of course, was all the new economic development in British hands. Old Indian firms could now enjoy that security throughout all India which in the days of anarchy they had only enjoyed within the British settlements: rich Parsi merchants in Bombay, rich Hindu merchants in Calcutta, grew richer still; and in course of time the Indian business world, aided by the experience and technique of British pioneers, was able both to launch out on its own and also to obtain an increasing share in the control and the profits of British firms. To-day the major part of the capital invested in joint-stock companies is passing from British into Indian hands.

One result of the new economic order was a steady rise in the value of India's export trade. In 1834 it had been under £8 millions. In 1855 it was roughly £23 millions, in 1870 £53, in 1900 £69, in 1910 £137, in 1928 £250. The goods exported were now mostly primary products — jute, cotton, grains and pulse, hides, oil-seeds, minerals — for India had been caught in the economic currents which the Industrial Revolution in the West had sent running all over the world. In the old days Indian yarns and calico, mainly produced by village craftsmen, had been exchanged for British bullion. Now in India, as earlier in Britain, village industries were doomed to a swift and steep decline by the growth of the factories. This would presumably have been their fate if the British had never come to India. Indian capitalism was not imported from abroad, and sooner or later Indian capitalists would have built the mills which now supply most of the cloth that Indians need. But, till that happened, it was mainly British yarn or cloth that swamped the Indian market. Other manufactures were also pouring in, not only the lighter goods, but the heavy stuff needed for the railways and other engineering works and presently for the equipment of Indian industry. Hence the value of India's imports rose beside that of the exports. In 1834 it was roughly £4½ millions, in 1855 £13½, in 1870 £33½, in 1900 £51, in 1910 £86, in 1928 £190.

The volume of British trade with India in this period ranged between one-fifth and one-seventh of the volume of all Britain's overseas trade, and it constituted a much larger share of India's overseas trade than that enjoyed by any other nation. This was the "natural" result of the Raj — of the connexion it had established between India and Britain, of the use of the English language it promoted, of its linking up of Indian with British currency, and so forth. It was not the result of any "unnatural" aids or restrictions. No more in the nineteenth than in the seventeenth century was there any attempt at a monopoly. Nor did the British Government — with one exception to be noted presently — try to foster British trade by such means as most other Western Governments have employed to foster their trade with backward countries under their control. . . .

For most of this period it was generally held that India benefited from British homage to the doctrine of Free Trade. It meant cheap rates for the consumer. The free import of Lancashire cotton goods, for example, from 1882 to 1894 enabled Indian countryfolk to obtain better material than they could get at the same price from Indian mills. But it was realised, as time went on, that the need for industrial development was only second to the need for the improvement of agricultural technique to provide the means of livelihood for a growing population; and in India large-scale industrial development was impossible without fiscal protection against the overwhelming flood of Western goods. The situation, in fact, was similar to that which had arisen at about the same time in those "young" countries of the British Commonwealth which were not content to exchange their corn and meat and dairy produce for European manufactures and wanted to create a better balance of their economic life by manufacturing themselves. But there was a vital difference. The concession of responsible government to those countries meant that on any issue of direct domestic concern they could have their own way. When, for example, in 1858-9 the Canadian Finance Minister raised his tariff in order to protect the infant industries of Canada from British and American competition, he met the protests of the British Colonial Secretary, backed by British manufacturers, with the firm assertion that a self-governing Canada must govern herself. A self-governing India would certainly have taken the same line.

India was to obtain her fiscal autonomy in course of time, but not before the difference in her political status had been harshly underlined by the sorry business of the excise duties. When the old low revenue-tariff was restored in 1894, the Lancashire manufacturers, who sent one-quarter of their cotton-goods to India, insisted that a countervailing excise must be levied on the products of Indian cotton-mills. They appealed to the principle of free competition, but they could not argue, as the Free Trade statesmen of an earlier day had honestly argued, that their policy was as much in the interests of Indian consumers as of British producers. On that point the British authorities in India had no doubts; but, at a time when the balance of parties in the House of Commons was fairly even, the voting power of the Lancashire members proved decisive, and Governor-General Elgin and his colleagues were overruled — one of the very few occasions on which such overruling from Whitehall has occurred in a matter of first-rate importance. The final upshot was the reduction of the import duty on cloth to 3½ per cent, the imposition of an excise duty of 3½ per cent on all cloth produced in Indian mills, and the exemption of yarn from both import and excise duties. It was a short-sighted policy, for it did more than anything else to strengthen Indian distrust of British motives and impair the goodwill on which in the long run all trade depends.[5]

At the time the duties were imposed, the political situation which made it possible had already begun to change; and a few

years later, as will be recorded in a subsequent chapter, India began to tread the Colonial path towards self-government. In 1917 the development of responsible government was declared to be the aim of British policy, and soon afterwards, as if in anticipation of its ultimate issue in Dominion status, India was conceded a substantial measure of fiscal autonomy. The immediate result was the erection of a discriminatory protective tariff. It was naturally directed, like the Canadian tariff, at British no less than foreign imports — in combination with the raising of revenue duties after the war, it ruined several firms in Lancashire and threw thousands of operatives out of work — and under its shield the pace of the industrial development which was already afoot soon quickened. In 1890 there were only some 700 registered factories in India. In 1939 there were over 10,000, employing nearly two million workers. And they were not only engaged on cotton, jute, leather, ceramics, and a multitude of light goods but in heavy industry too. The Tata Company, financed and controlled by Indians and fed with Indian ore and Indian coal, began to produce steel in 1912, and it now produces more steel and iron than any other firm in any part of the British Empire — a portent of great significance for the future of Asia.

One other feature of the new dispensation calls for mention. It was agreed in 1921 that in the making of Government purchases overseas India could not be treated as "a tied-house for British industry" and that such purchases should be made in the cheapest market. Substantial orders were subsequently placed in continental European countries — an order for locomotives in Germany, for example. In 1935, 51 per cent of India's imports came from foreign countries and 39 per cent from Britain, and 54 per cent of India's exports went to foreign countries and 31½ per cent to Britain — the residue in each case falling to other parts of the British Empire. As far, then, as fiscal policy is concerned and save only in that matter of the excise duties, the

[5] The import duties on cotton goods were presently raised to 11 per cent, while the excise duty remained at 3½. The latter was suspended in 1925 and abolished in 1926.

British Raj cannot fairly be branded as an example of "economic imperialism."

2. *Public Finance.* The poverty of the Indian people is betrayed by the relatively small amount of money that can be raised from them by taxation. In 1932, for example, the revenue of Britain with a population of about 45 millions was about £870 millions; the revenue of British India — Central and Provincial together — with a population of nearly 300 millions was about £160 millions.

That great system of railways and canals could never have been financed from such a relatively meagre revenue. Loans were plainly needed, and they were obtained by issues of Government of India stock on the British and the Indian market. The former was known as "sterling debt," the latter as "rupee debt." Up to the outbreak of the last war, the average rate of interest on both was only about 3½ per cent, because Indian administration was under the ultimate control of the Secretary of State and Parliament. Japan, for instance, could not hope to get such favourable terms: the average charge on her overseas public debt was 5½ per cent. Moreover, the debt incurred on the railways (most of which were built by private companies with a Government guarantee to begin with, but were successively bought up by Government in course of time) and on the canals (which, apart from one or two minor and unsuccessful private ventures, were a Government concern from the outset) proved to be "productive" debt. The canals quite soon, the railways more slowly, began to yield profits higher than the interest charges. Thus India has been in a fortunate position with regard to the bulk of her National Debt — an almost unique position, since few other countries can have such a very high proportion of their public debt secured by productive assets — and it has been still further improved in the course of the present war. The "sterling debt," the part owed to Britain, which amounted in 1937 to £357 millions,[6]

[6] Including railway liabilities taken over by the Secretary of State.

has now been "repatriated" against the sterling received on account of the British Government's large expenditure for war purposes in India. The financial roles have thus been reversed. Owing to the cost of the war in South-East Asia, Britain is now heavily in debt to India.

The normal requirements of administration could not be met so easily by loans; and, if much has been left undone that wanted doing, the main reason has been that there was not money enough to do it. The chief source of revenue, till twenty years ago, was the land. The British Government inherited from the Indian rulers they supplanted the traditional right to acquire, as ultimate owners of the soil, a proportion of its yield. This rent or tax had normally been levied in kind — one-third of the gross produce was a customary rate under the later Moguls — but it was now all levied in cash; and for this purpose an elaborate process of assessment and periodical re-assessment was carried out. At the end of the nineteenth century it was roughly reckoned that the average tax on an acre was not more than one-tenth of the value of its yield or about two shillings a year. . . .

The heaviest item of expenditure has always been defence. The Indian Army — in which the Company's sepoy troops were consolidated and reorganised — was maintained at a peace-time strength of about 150,000. Its main task has been the protection of the north-west frontier against the sturdy, fanatical and bellicose Pathans who had been accustomed in earlier days to make up for the poverty of their rocky hill-country by raiding the plains along the Indus. Intermittent warfare was unavoidable, but the frequency of costly little frontier campaigns became a matter of controversy both between those British experts who held different views as to the line on which the frontier should be stabilised and between Indian nationalists and the British Government. But the sharpest criticism of defence policy was the use it made of the Indian Army outside India. Between 1858 and 1914 Indian troops served on a large scale in the second Afghan War (1878–80) and the third Burman War (1885), and on a smaller scale in Perak (1875), in Egypt (1882), in the Sudan (1885 and 1896), in South Africa (1899–1902) and in China (1900–1). To Indian critics it seemed that, in some of those cases at any rate, the defence of India was only distantly or indirectly involved, and in course of time it became a common charge that Indian lives were sacrificed to "imperial adventures." And Indian money too: for the cost of the Indian troops on the earlier of those campaigns was borne by Indian tax-payers.[7] In the World Wars of our own day the security of India has been directly threatened, and her contributions to their cost (about £140 millions in the first war, a vastly larger sum in the second) have been contributions to her own self-defence. At the same time, in each of the two wars, the maintenance of the Indian Army outside India has been paid for by the British Government. Shortly before 1939, moreover, the British Government undertook to bear three-quarters of the cost of modernising and mechanising the Indian Army or about £25 millions. It must also be borne in mind that India paid only a relatively small subsidy (about £130,000 a year) towards the cost of the protection to her shores and trade afforded by the British Navy. The self-governing Colonies had paid such subsidies before they attained Dominion Status and built up their own navies; and in 1938, in accordance with Dominion precedent, India ceased to pay the subsidy on undertaking to establish a squadron of modern ships.

On the eve of the recent war the propor-

[7] Indian nationalists also complained that the cost of recruiting and training British troops before they were stationed in India for its defence was charged on Indian revenues. This matter was settled in 1933 when the British Government undertook to pay £1½ millions (raised in 1939 to £2 millions) in relief of Indian defence expenditure on the ground that (*a*) the British forces in India were ready for action in an emergency, especially in the Far East, and (*b*) they obtained in India a training for active service unobtainable elsewhere.

tion of total British Indian revenues spent on defence was no longer quite so high as it had been in the nineteenth century, but it was still about 25 per cent. When the cost of administrative salaries and pensions and of debt charges and of roads and bridges and other public works was added, there was no room for high expenditure on social services. In education, for example, an attempt by the State to do in India what it had begun to do in Europe in the later nineteenth century would have entailed an outlay far beyond its means. A good deal was done. There are now fifteen universities in India, over 300 colleges, over 3,000 high schools. In 1939 over eleven million children were attending primary schools. But a system of universal primary education — the provision and upkeep of innumerable village schools, the training and payment of a host of teachers in the various vernaculars — has been financially impossible. The cost would have run into hundreds of millions sterling, and the amount assigned to education from public funds in 1939 was about £13 millions.

Economists are now maintaining that public expenditure need not be determined by the taxable capacity of the people; but this is a novel doctrine, and hitherto British control of Indian, as of British, finance has been strictly orthodox. Budgets have been balanced. "Cut thy coat according to thy cloth" has been the motto. Borrowing, except for "productive" purposes, has been severely restricted. And on those assumptions it has never been possible to achieve a better counterpoise between the cost of defence and administration and the cost of social services. It is arguable, indeed, that India under the British Raj has obtained a more highly organised system of defence than was necessary, and a more efficient and elaborate administration than so poor and backward a country could properly afford.

3. *The Problem of Poverty*. The closer association of India with the commerce of the world, the great increase in her total production and in the volume of her export

and import trade, the ultimate development of industries — all this should seemingly have meant a corresponding advance in the general standard of living. But it did not. For several reasons the mass of the Indian people remained desperately poor. In the first place the growth of population, no longer checked by constant warfare and anarchy and disease and recurrent famine, steadily quickened. Between 1881 and 1931 the population of all India increased by about 85 millions. At the census of 1941 it was nearly 390 millions. It is over 400 by now, and climbing higher at the rate of five or six millions a year. That is a highly disquieting fact because the increase in the number of people has not been accompanied, as in the Western world, by a corresponding increase in their productive capacity per head. That is the primary reason why the great majority of them are still near to that bare subsistence level at which they stood a century ago.

But why, it will be asked, did productive capacity remain so stunted? The answer to that question is more complex. It was partly due to the slow and relatively slight development of large-scale industry, the means by which the prosperous countries of the West were able to absorb their growing populations and to increase the value of their individual output. But India could never have become a predominantly industrial country like Britain or Belgium: the bulk of her people had to be employed on the land; and in the last analysis the economic backwardness of India is inseparable from the backwardness of Indian agriculture. For that, unhappily, there was no easy remedy. For it was not only due to the ignorance and conservatism of the Indian peasant or to insecure tenures and inequitable rents in those parts of the country in which "landlordism" still prevailed, or to the customary "fragmentation" of agricultural holdings. It was also due to the rigid traditions of Indian society. If caste and the Hindu family system encourage fellowship and mutual help between their mem-

bers, they also tend to discourage individual initiative; and there is no economic activity in India that has not been impaired, directly or indirectly, by the seclusion and subordination of women, both Moslem and Hindu. The custom, again, of costly marriage ceremonies and high dowries has involved the Hindu peasant in a load of debt so strangling that most of what he can produce above the mere means of life is appropriated by the moneylender — a fate to which the Moslem peasant, too, has usually succumbed. Religion, also, has obstructed progress: the Hindu veneration of the cow virtually prohibits the development of a successful pastoral industry. And behind those checks and drawbacks of Indian creed and custom lies the lack of vitality due to disease and an insufficient or ill-balanced diet.

But, when all is said, the main cause of Indian poverty remains the high birth-rate. More Indians have been born than India could comfortably maintain. All the efforts that have been made to enhance productive capacity — by irrigation, by improvements in agricultural technique, by sanitation, by industrial development — have been swamped by the rising flood of human beings; and it is hard to believe that the far-reaching schemes now being canvassed for raising the standard of Indian life can prove more than partially successful unless somehow the birth-rate is reduced.

It is clear from the foregoing that it lay beyond the power of an alien Government to grapple with the root causes of Indian poverty. It might have done more to hasten the growth of industry. It might have done more to protect the tenant from the landlord and the moneylender. But, being an alien Government, it could not launch a direct attack on the religious convictions or social traditions or domestic habits of its subjects. That is one reason for welcoming the transfer of political power from British to Indian hands if it can be safely and honourably made: for the change of methods and habits and outlook on life among the multitude of Indian countryfolk, without which India can never be prosperous, must be the work of Indians.

BALANCE SHEET

1. *Gain and Loss.* The connexion between Britain and India has been much more than a matter of politics and economics. It has furnished an example of "culture contact" on a vast scale; and, though the influence of British political ideas on Indian minds can be easily detected and defined, the same cannot be said about the impact on Indian life of all that is meant by Western civilisation or the counter-reaction of Indian on British thought or the effect of the personal relations between innumerable Britons and Indians. A scientific attempt, indeed, to assess the worth of the British Raj to each of the two countries would involve so many imponderable factors that it might well daunt the most self-confident investigator. The whole subject, moreover, is nowadays highly controversial. For a long time to come no two verdicts, especially if one is British and the other Indian, are likely to be the same. However objective they may try to be, British and Indian patriots must view the picture from different angles and be affected in some degree by an inescapable, if unconscious, bias. Yet some judgment, however rough and cursory and limited in scope, must needs be ventured here: for no one can understand the theme of the forthcoming chapters — the process of India's liberation — unless he has formed some opinion as to the nature and results of India's subjection and the gains and losses it has involved for both the countries concerned.

The British balance sheet is the easier to compile. Nearly all the main items are on the credit side, and their value is indisputable. First, the British occupation of India has provided a strategic base, protecting the "life-line" of the Empire, by sea and air, across the Indian Ocean from Aden to Singapore and on to Australia and New Zealand. Secondly, India has been one of the safest fields of British overseas invest-ment and trade. Thirdly, though, as has just been said, the effect of the connexion between Britain and India on the culture of each country cannot be precisely measured and though it has clearly been much stronger and more pervasive in India, yet it has been by no means negligible in Britain. The modern sciences of comparative philology and comparative religion were founded on the study of the Hindu classics. British archaeologists and historians have quarried in Indian soil; and British literature and art have been more influenced than is generally realised by Indian poetry, painting and sculpture. Fourthly, the Raj has offered to successive generations of young Englishmen an attractive, honourable and well-paid career in the Indian civil and military services. Against that last item must be set the loss which British life has suffered, in administration and politics, in the professions and business, through the exile of so much ability and integrity and capacity for leadership. But otherwise there is nothing substantial to put on the debit side. The Raj has certainly fulfilled the first of the two purposes which Pitt assigned to it in 1784 — "to confirm and enlarge the advantages derived by this country from its connexion with India." And in so far as it has also fulfilled the second purpose — "to render that connexion a blessing to the native Indians" — there has been moral as well as material gain. Since the days when Burke told them that they had a duty to do in India, the British people have certainly tried to do it. "Few governments," wrote J. S. Mill, who was no chauvinist, "have attempted so much for the good of their subjects";[8] and much more has been attempted since Mill's day than was conceivable before it. There have been shortcomings, of course, and blunders; but it is the general British belief, and it has become part of the British national tradition, that the record of the Raj, though it has one or two black pages, is on the whole

[8] *Parliamentary Papers,* 1857–8, xliii. 35.

a record of which the British people have sober reason to be proud. Whatever may be said in the dust and heat of recent controversy, they need not fear the eventual verdict of cold history.

The major benefits which the Raj has bestowed on India are also plain. First and foremost, it has not only safeguarded India, as never before, from recurrent attack from without; it has also given her that internal unity, political and economic, which is the natural response to her physical unity, but which for centuries past she had never attained for any length of time. Secondly, British rule has been the rule of law. It has protected the rights of individuals and communities more fully and impartially than any previous régime, and fostered a sense of allegiance to the sovereignty of law. Thirdly, it has brought the economic life of India out of its almost medieval isolation into the network of modern world-economy; and the material profit of this revolution, though much of it has been taken by British business and though it has not much relieved the poverty of the great rural majority of the Indian people, has been increasingly shared by all other classes of Indian society. Fourthly, the closer connexion with the West involved in British rule has made it easier for the Indian intelligentsia to draw, for what it was worth to them, on the storehouse of Western culture, the science, philosophy, art and literature of all the Western world.[9]

So much for the credit side of the account. On the debit side stand all the disadvantages inherent in the one hard fact that British rule has been foreign rule.

2. *The Nationalist Audit.* It is only in relatively recent times that India's political subjection has come to be regarded by most Indian politicians as completely upsetting the balance of gain and loss to India resulting from the British Raj. Till some sixty years ago the drawbacks of foreign rule seemed outweighed by the benefits it

brought with it, and not least the opportunity it gave to Indians to outgrow it and dispense with it by providing the framework and the training needed for self-government. At one time, indeed, educated Indian opinion may be said to have been too pro-British. It was not only in politics that the British way of doing things was accepted as the obvious model for an inexperienced India: there was a tendency to decry the whole historic tradition of Indian life and thought and to hold that India could only recover her place in the world by turning her back on her past and acquiring to the fullest possible extent the practical virtues of the West. This soon provoked a healthy reaction, but there were other reasons for the growth of a more critical appraisement of the British Raj. In the first place the value of its greatest gifts — external security and internal unity — was apt to be forgotten or underestimated as the conditions of Indian life before the British took control faded from living memory. The peril of invasion was no more thought about in India than in Britain till the catastrophes of 1940 and 1942 brought it so sensationally near. It needed, similarly, the widening of the communal gulf after 1937, the raising of the banner of Pakistan, the sombre talk of civil war, to recall the disruption and anarchy which preceded the British Raj. The *Pax Britannica*, in fact, external and internal, was taken for granted, and it was not recognised that united India, since the Mutiny at any rate, had escaped the fate of disunited India, smitten by constant war and exposed in peace to the assaults of economic nationalism. The second reason for a change of attitude towards the British Raj went deeper. It was not so much forgetfulness of what it had given to India as a new awareness of what it had not given. With the growth of Indian nationalism — itself (as will be explained later on) made possible by the Raj — there was bound to grow a feeling of impatience with the notion of training for self-government. Quickened by the gathering strength of nationalism all over the world and particu-

[9] On this point, as indeed on all points, it is instructive to compare what happened in subject India with what happened in free China.

larly by its struggles and successes in other Asiatic countries in the opening decades of the twentieth century, this impatience soon became the dominant emotion in the hearts of most educated Indians. Freedom as a far-off goal was no longer enough. They wanted it not only for their sons but for themselves. And it was not so much with the backward state of India that they felt impatient now: it was with the British Raj. Once regarded as the means of attaining self-government, it seemed now the only obstacle that barred the way to it.

This intensification of nationalist feeling unhappily gave a new importance to what has been the most regrettable feature of the Raj. It is one of the major problems of world society, not by any means confined to India, that white men often find it hard not to feel and to betray a sense of superiority to coloured men. It is particularly hard where the white men are the rulers and the coloured men are subject to their rule. And it stands to the credit of those Englishmen who, holding the higher posts in the administration, have been the actual rulers in India that, with few exceptions, in their personal relations with Indians they have — to use a phrase that has not yet lost its meaning — behaved like gentlemen. If, being British, they have been stiff and undemonstrative and have tended to keep themselves to themselves, there have been many cases of close and equal friendship between them and their Indian colleagues. Outside official circles, too, strong personal ties have been knit — between officers of the Indian Army and their subordinates, between teachers and pupils, between partners in work or play. Nor have these good traditions been seriously impaired by the growth of Indian nationalism and the bitter hostility with which its spokesmen have from time to time assailed the British record. Often, indeed, those Englishmen who have least sympathised with Indian aspirations have been most considerate of Indian feelings. Unfortunately, however, Englishmen in India have not all been gentlemen, whether by upbringing or nature; too many

of them — and of Englishwomen also — have claimed from Indians, whatever their respective stations in life, a deference inconceivable on any grounds but those of race and, worse still, have sometimes enforced the claim with unpardonable insolence. Such conduct, it need hardly be said, has always been sternly reprobated by the authorities; but public opinion in the British community at large has failed to make it impossible for such things to happen; and there was one notorious occasion on which the lesson in race-relations taught by those petty individual incidents was driven home collectively. In 1883, when the liberal-minded Governor-General Ripon sponsored a bill which made it possible for a British resident in India to be tried by an Indian for a criminal offence, the storm raised by the unofficial British community was so violent that Ripon was constrained to bow to it and amend the bill. No doubt, in all the circumstances, some such agitation was inevitable — there have been similar reactions to similar situations in other parts of the world — but few of those who took part in it seem to have realised or cared what conclusions educated Indians were bound to draw.

Such demonstrations of a claim to racial superiority became more intolerable as nationalism strengthened its hold on Indian minds. For the principle of equal status for all nations, great and small, is the cardinal doctrine of nationalism in revolt; and the main reason why an Indian patriot longs for India's freedom is that he resents the inferior position which, despite her ancient civilisation and historic past, she now occupies in the society of nations. If this is natural, so also is the patriot's tendency to shy away from the plain fact that that inferior position must needs have been the result, in some degree at any rate, of Indian weaknesses. Naturally, too, a sense of wounded pride may carry him further. He may persuade himself that India was enjoying a millennium before the British came and that her failure to take her due place in the modern world as a free, united, prosperous nation has been Britain's fault. It is this attitude of mind, more emotional than realistic, that accounts for the transformation of the old ideas about the British Raj in the course of the last fifty years. The balance sheet was re-audited; and now the items on the credit side seemed not only dwarfed by the one great debit item of subjection, their intrinsic value was questioned and written down. India, no doubt, had been protected from invasion, but at an unbearable cost. The British, no doubt, united India, but this was the almost automatic result of the development of modern transport which synchronised with the growth of British rule. That communal peace had been imposed by a neutral British administration was an illusion. The Hindu-Moslem gulf, in particular, had grown wider; the British indeed, it was ultimately asserted, had deliberately widened it on the principle of "divide and rule." If the economic development of India was mainly Britain's work, its profits had gone mainly into British pockets; and India had been impoverished by the steady "drain" of wealth to Britain — the salaries and pensions of British civilians and officers, the debt charges, the proceeds of British business — and by what was called "the 'City's' stranglehold on high finance." Embittered patriots came to believe that it would have been better that India's natural resources should have lain untouched and undeveloped until Indians had acquired the capacity to exploit them entirely by themselves. And the reaction penetrated finally into the realm of culture. Contact with Western materialism had soiled the spiritual texture of Indian thought and life. Even the English language had been no boon. It was as harmful as it was degrading for a country which had been civilised ages before Europe to adopt a foreign *lingua franca* for its multilingual people.[10] To cool-headed observers there seemed to be a good deal of exaggeration and make-believe in this revaluation of the British Raj. But not all Indian nationalists were cool-headed. Some of them, indeed, came to feel in the end so acute a sense of humiliation and impotence that any fate for India — disruption, civil war, chaos — seemed preferable to the continuation of the Raj.

The reaction could go no further, but it must not be supposed that all Indian patriots went so far. Many of them, while desiring no less ardently that India should be free, regarded her subjection as not insufferable because it was not to be permanent. Their attitude to the British Raj would doubtless have been the same as that of the more militant nationalists if Britain had not been true to her liberal tradition and set on foot a gradual process of constitutional advance which, sooner or later, would lead to full self-government. As it was, they saw the process moving, slowly at first, but presently with gathering momentum, till at last only one short stretch lay between them and their goal. Plainly, it seemed to them, the revolutionists' cry that Britain was tightening her "imperial grip" on India was false: plainly she was loosening it.

[10] In an address at Benares University in 1942 Mr. Gandhi praised the Japanese for "learning the best of the West through their own language." *Leader*, 23 January 1942.

The Exploitation of India: A Marxist View

R. PALME DUTT

Rajani Palme Dutt (1896–) was born in Cambridge, England, of Indian-Swedish parentage. Educated at Oxford University, he founded *Labour Monthly* in 1921 and has been its editor ever since. He has been a member of the executive committee of the Communist Party of Great Britain since 1922. He is the author of *Fascism and Social Revolution* (1934), *World Politics, 1918–1936* (1936), and *The Crisis of Britain and the British Empire* (1953), but his best known work is *India Today* (1940), from which the following selection is taken.

THREE main periods stand out in this history of imperialist rule in India. The first is the period of Merchant-Capital, represented by the East India Company, and extending in the general character of its system to the end of the eighteenth century. The second is the period of Industrial Capital which established a new basis of exploitation of India in the nineteenth century. The third is the modern period of Finance-Capital, developing its distinctive system of the exploitation of India on the remains of the old, and growing up from its first beginnings in the closing years of the nineteenth century to its fuller development in the most recent phase. . . .

We may therefore cover in summary fashion the first two stages, which are of primary importance as laying the basis for the present system, and for understanding the line of development to the present situation, in order then to concentrate mainly on the modern development.[1]

The era of the East India Company is conventionally measured from its first Char-

ter in 1600 to its final merging in the Crown in 1858. In fact its main period of domination of India was the second half of the eighteenth century. . . .

By the middle of the eighteenth century the Company began to build up its territorial power in India. The internal wars which racked India in the eighteenth century after the decline of the Moghul Empire represented a period of inner confusion (comparable in some respects to the Wars of the Roses in England or the Thirty Years War in Germany) necessary for the break-up of the old order and preparing the way, in the normal course of evolution, for the rise of bourgeois power on the basis of the advancing merchant, shipping and manufacturing interests in Indian society. The invasion, however, during this critical period of the representatives of the more highly developed European bourgeoisie, with their superior technical and military equipment and social-political cohesion, thwarted this normal course of evolution, and led to the outcome that the bourgeois rule which supervened in India on the break-up of the old order was not Indian bourgeois rule, growing up within the shell of the old order, but foreign bourgeois rule, forcibly superimposing itself on the old society and smashing the germs of the rising

[1] For much of the material in this chapter special indebtedness should be expressed to R. C. Dutt's "Economic History of India under Early British Rule" (1901) and "Economic History of India in the Victorian Age" (1903), which remain the most authoritative studies on the development up to the end of the 19th century.

From Rajani Palme Dutt, *India Today* (2nd revised Indian edition; Bombay, 1949), pp. 94–102, 108–109, 112–114, 118–119, 123–137. By permission of the author.

41

Indian bourgeois class. Herein lay the tragedy of Indian development, which thereafter became a thwarted or distorted social development for the benefit of a foreign bourgeoisie. . . .

The decisive period of the East India Company's domination and special exploitation of India was the second half of the eighteenth century, the great germinal period of modern capitalism. The character of that exploitation differs from the subsequent nineteenth-century exploitation by industrial capital, and requires its separate analysis.

The original aim of the East India Company in its trade with India was the typical aim of the monopolist companies of Merchant Capital, to make a profit by securing a monopoly trade in the goods and products of an overseas country. The governing objective was, not the hunt for a market for British manufactures, but the endeavour to secure a supply of the products of India and the East Indies (especially spices, cotton goods and silk goods), which found a ready market in England and Europe, and could thus yield a rich profit on every successful expedition that could return with a supply.

The problem, however, which faced the Company from the outset was that, in order to secure these goods from India by way of trade, it was necessary to offer India something in exchange. England, at the stage of development reached in the early seventeenth century, had nothing of value to offer India in the way of products comparable in quality or technical standard with Indian products, the only important industry then developed being the manufacture of woollen goods, which were of no use for India. Therefore precious metals had to be taken out to buy the goods in India.

The whole difficulty of trading with the East lay in the fact that Europe had so little to send out that the East wanted — a few luxury articles for the Courts, lead, copper, quicksilver and tin, coral, gold and ivory, were the only commodities except silver that India would absorb. Therefore it was mainly silver that was taken out. (*L. C. A. Knowles, "Economic Development of the Overseas Empire," p. 73.*)

Accordingly, at its commencement the East India Company was given a special authorisation to export an annual value of £30,000 in silver, gold and foreign coin. But this was most painful and repugnant to the whole system of Mercantile Capitalism, which regarded the precious metals as the only real wealth a country could possess, and the essential object of trade as to secure a net favourable balance expressed in an influx of precious metals or increase of real wealth.

From the outset the merchant "adventurers" of the East India Company were much concerned to devise a means to solve this problem and secure the goods of India for little or no payment. One of their first devices was to develop a system of roundabout trade, and, in particular, to utilise the plunder from the rest of the colonial system, in Africa and America, to meet the costs in India, where they had not yet the power to plunder directly:

The English trade with India was really a chase to find something that India would be willing to take, and the silver obtained by the sale of the slaves in the West Indies and Spanish America was all-important in this connection. (*Knowles, op. cit., p. 74.*)

As soon, however, as domination began to be established in India, by the middle of the eighteenth century, methods of power could be increasingly used to weight the balance of exchange and secure the maximum goods for the minimum payment. The margin between trade and plunder, from the outset never very sharply drawn (the original "adventurers" often combined trade with piracy) began to grow conspicuously thin. The merchant, in any case always favourably placed in relation to the individual producer, whether weaver or peasant, to dictate terms favourable to himself, was now able to throw the sword into the scales to secure a bargain which abandoned all pretence of equality of exchange. By 1762 the Nawab of Bengal was complaining impotently to the Company about the Company's agents:

They forcibly take away the goods and commodities of the Ryots (peasants), merchants, etc., for a fourth part of their value; and by ways of violence and oppression they oblige the Ryots, etc., to give five rupees for goods which are worth but one rupee. (*Memorandum of the Nawab of Bengal to the English Governor, May, 1762.*)

Similarly an English merchant, William Bolts, in his "Considerations on India Affairs," published in 1772, described the process:

The English, with their Banyans and black Gomastahs [i.e., brokers and agents — Ed.] arbitrarily decide what quantities of goods each manufacturer shall deliver, and the prices he shall receive for them. . . . The assent of the poor weaver is in general not deemed necessary; for the Gomastahs, when employed on the Company's investment, frequently make them sign what they please; and upon the weavers refusing to take the money offered, it has been known that they have had it tied in their girdles, and they have been sent away with a flogging. . . . A number of these weavers are generally also registered in the books of the Company's Gomastahs, and not permitted to work for any others, being transferred from one to another as so many slaves. . . . The roguery practised in this department is beyond imagination; but all terminates in the defrauding of the poor weaver; for the prices which the Company's Gomastahs, and in confederacy with them the Jachendars (examiners of fabrics) fix upon the goods, are in all places at least 15 per cent, and some even 40 per cent less than the goods so manufactured would sell in the public bazaar or market upon free sale." (*William Bolts, "Considerations on India Affairs," 1772, pp. 191–4.*)

Nominal "trade" was thus already more plunder than trade.

But when the administration of the revenues passed into the hands of the Company, with the granting of the Dewani or civil administration of Bengal, Bihar and Orissa in 1765, a new field of limitless direct plunder was opened up in addition to the profits of "trade." Then began a process of wholesale unashamed spoliation which has made the Company's administration during the last third of the eighteenth century a by-word in history. . . .

What was the character of the system established by the East India Company when it had won the civil power in Bengal and in other territories it conquered? The direct calculation of the profit to be made and remitted to England as the sole consideration in taking over the administration was set out by Clive in his letter to the Directors in 1765 with a clearness and simplicity which are in refreshing contrast to subsequent philanthropic humbug:

Your revenues, by means of this acquisition, will, as near as I can judge, not fall far short for the ensuing year of 250 lakhs of Sicca Rupees, including your former possessions of Burdwan, etc. Hereafter they will at least amount to 20 or 30 lakhs more. Your civil and military expenses in time of peace can never exceed 60 lakhs of Rupees; the Nabob's allowances are already reduced to 42 lakhs, and the tribute to the King (the Great Mogul) at 26; so that there will be remaining a clear gain to the Company of 122 lakhs of Sicca Rupees or £1,650,900 sterling. (*Clive, letter to the Directors of the East India Company, September 30, 1765.*)

Here all is as straightforward and businesslike as a merchant's ledger. Of the total revenue extracted from the population one quarter is considered sufficient for the purposes of government; one quarter is still needed to square the claims of the local potentates (Nabob and Mogul); the remainder, or half the revenue, estimated at £1½ million, is "clear gain." Bottomley's old dream of the "Business Man's Government" is here realised with a completeness never equalled before or since.

How far the results achieved corresponded to the aims is shown by the statement of the revenues and expenses of Bengal during the first six years of the Company's administration, as reported to Parliament in 1773. The total net revenue was given as £13,066,761; the total expenditure as £9,027,609; the balance of £4,037,152 was remitted. Thus nearly one-third of the revenues of Bengal was sent out of the country as "clear gain."

But this was by no means the total of the tribute. Enormous fortunes were made by individual officers of the Company. Clive himself, who started from nothing, returned home with a fortune estimated at a quarter of a million pounds, in addition to an Indian estate bringing in £27,000 a year; he reported that "fortunes of £100,000 have been obtained in two years." A measure closer to the full tribute is revealed by the figures of exports and imports; during the three years 1766–68, according to the report of the Governor, Verelst, exports amounted to £6,311,250, while imports amounted to only £624,375. Thus ten times as much was taken out of the country as was sent into it under the ruling care of this new type of merchant company governing a country.

The dearest dream of the merchants of the East India Company was thus realised: to draw the wealth out of India without having to send wealth in return. As a member of Clive's Council, L. Scrafton, exulted already in 1763, on the basis of the initial stages of spoliation achieved after Plassey, it had been possible for three years to carry on the whole India trade "without sending out one ounce of bullion":

These glorious successes have brought near three millions of money to the nation; for, properly speaking, almost the whole of the immense sums received from the Soubah finally centres in England. So great a proportion of it fell into the Company's hands, either from their own share, or by sums paid into the treasury at Calcutta for bills and receipts, that they have been enabled to carry on the whole trade of India (China excepted) for three years together, without sending out one ounce of bullion. Vast sums have been also remitted through the hands of foreign companies, which weigh in the balance of trade to their amount in our favour with such foreign nations. (L. Scrafton, "Reflections on the Government of Indostan," 1763.)

The portion of the revenues of Bengal which was remitted to England was termed, by a judiciously inverted terminology, the Company's "investment." On this system the Select Committee of the House of Commons reported in 1783:

A certain portion of the revenues of Bengal has been for many years set apart in the purchase of goods for exportation to England, and this is called the Investment. The greatness of this Investment has been the standard by which the merit of the Company's principal servants has been too generally estimated; and this main cause of the impoverishment of India has been generally taken as a measure of its wealth and prosperity. . . . But the payment of a tribute, and not a beneficial commerce to that country, wore this specious and delusive appearance. . . .

When an account is taken of the intercourse, for it is not commerce, which is carried on between Bengal and England, the pernicious effects of the system of Investment from revenue will appear in the strongest point of view. In that view, the whole exported produce of the country, so far as the Company is concerned, is not exchanged in the course of barter, but it is taken away without any return or payment whatever. ("House of Commons Select Committee's Ninth Report," 1783, pp. 54–5.)

The effects of this system on the population of Bengal can be imagined. The ceaselessly renewed demand for more and yet more spoils led to the most reckless raising of the land revenue demands to heights which in many cases even meant taking the seed corn and the bullocks from the peasants. . . .

The spoliation of India was the hidden source of accumulation which played an all-important role in helping to make possible the Industrial Revolution in England.

But once the Industrial Revolution had been achieved in England with the aid of plunder of India, the new task became to find adequate outlets for the flood of manufactured goods. This necessitated a revolution in the economic system, from the principles of mercantile capitalism to the principles of free-trade capitalism. And this in turn involved a corresponding complete change in the methods of the colonial system.

The new needs required the creation of a free market in India in place of the previous monopoly. It became necessary to transform India from an exporter of cotton goods to the whole world into an importer of cotton goods. This meant a revolution in the economy of India. It meant at the same time a complete changeover from the whole previous system of the East India Company. A transformation had to be carried through in the methods of exploitation of India, and a transformation that would have to be fought through against the strenuous opposition of the vested interests of the Company's monopoly.

The first steps preparing the way for this change had already been undertaken in the last decade and a half of the eighteenth century.

It was obvious that, in the interests of effective exploitation, the wholesale anarchic and destructive methods of spoliation pursued by the East India Company and its servants could not continue without some change. The stupid and reckless rapacity of the Company and its servants was destroying the basis of exploitation, just as in England a few years later the unbounded greed of the Lancashire manufacturers was to devour nine generations of the people in one. And just as the greed of the manufacturers had to be curbed by the action of the State on behalf of the capitalist class as a whole, in the interests of future exploitation (the attack being led by their economic rivals, the landed interests), so in the last quarter of the eighteenth century the central organs of the State had to be invoked to regulate the operations of the Company in India. Here also the attack was led by the rival interests. All the nu-

merous interests opposed to the exclusive monopoly of the East India Company combined to organise a powerful offensive against it. From this offensive arose a vast literature of opposition during this period against the misgovernment of the East India Company, a literature of opposition which, for completeness, detail and authority, is without equal in the exposure of imperialism at any time. . . .

In 1813 the offensive of the industrialists and other trading interests was at last successful, and the monopoly of the East India Company in trade with India was ended. The new stage of industrial capitalist exploitation of India may thus be dated from 1813.

Prior to 1813 trade with India had been relatively small. . . . The official Report of the Company in 1812 made clear that the value of India at that time was as a source of direct tribute or spoliation, not as a market for goods:

The importance of that immense Empire to this country is rather to be estimated by the great annual addition it makes to the wealth and capital of the Kingdom, than by any eminent advantage which the manufacturers of the country can derive from the consumption of the natives of India. (*Report of the East India Company for 1812*, quoted in Parshad, "Some Aspects of India's Foreign Trade," p. 49.)

The proceedings of the parliamentary enquiry of 1813, preceding the renewal of the Charter and abolition of the monopoly, showed how completely the current of thought was now directed to the new aim of the development of India as a market for the rising British machine industry. It was further notable how the replies of the representatives of the old school, like Warren Hastings, denied the possibility of the development of India as a market.

At the time of this enquiry, the duties on the import of Indian calicoes into Britain were 78 per cent. Without these prohibitive duties the British cotton industry could not have developed in its early stages.

It was stated in evidence (in 1813) that the cotton and silk goods of India up to the period could be sold for a profit in the British market at a price from 50% to 60% lower than those fabricated in England. It consequently became necessary to protect the latter by duties of 70% and 80% on their value, or by positive prohibition. Had this not been the case, had not such prohibitory duties and decrees existed, the mills of Paisley and Manchester would have been stopped in their outset, and could scarcely have been again set in motion, even by the power of steam. They were created by the sacrifice of the Indian manufacture. (*H. H. Wilson, "History of British India," Vol. I, p. 385.*)

This tariff discrimination against Indian manufactures to build up the British textile industry was carried on in the first half of the nineteenth century. In the parliamentary enquiry of 1840 it was reported that, while British cotton and silk goods imported into India paid a duty of 3½ per cent and woollen goods 2 per cent, Indian cotton goods imported into Britain paid 10 per cent, silk goods 20 per cent and woollen goods 30 per cent.

Thus it was not only on the basis of the technical superiority of machine industry, but also with the direct State assistance of one-way free trade (free entry, or virtual free entry, for British goods into India, but tariffs against the entry of Indian manufactures into Britain, and prevention of direct trade between India and European or rather foreign countries by the operation of the Navigation Acts) that the predominance of British manufactures was built up in the Indian market and the Indian manufacturing industries were destroyed.

This process was decisively carried through in the first half of the nineteenth century, although its effects continued to operate right through the nineteenth century and even into the twentieth century. Alongside the headlong advance of British manufactures went the decline of Indian manufactures.

Between 1814 and 1835 British cotton manufactures exported to India rose from less than 1 million yards to over 51 million yards. In the same period Indian cotton piecegoods imported into Britain fell from one and a quarter million pieces to 306,000 pieces, and by 1844 to 63,000 pieces.

The contrast in values is no less striking. Between 1815 and 1832 the value of Indian cotton goods exported fell from £1.3 million to below £100,000, or a loss of twelve-thirteenths of the trade in seventeen years. In the same period the value of English cotton goods imported into India rose from £26,000 to £400,000, or an increase of sixteen times. By 1850 India, which had for centuries exported cotton goods to the whole world, was importing one-fourth of all British cotton exports.

While machine-made cotton goods from England ruined the weavers, machine-made twist ruined the spinners. Between 1818 and 1836 the export of cotton twist from England to India rose 5,200 times.

The same process could be traced in respect of silk goods, woollen goods, iron, pottery, glass and paper.

The effects of this wholesale destruction of the Indian manufacturing industries on the economy of the country can be imagined. In England the ruin of the old handloom weavers was accompanied by the growth of the new machine industry. But in India the ruin of the millions of artisans and craftsmen was not accompanied by any alternative growth of new forms of industry. . . .

The industrial capitalists had their policy for India clearly defined: to make India the agricultural colony of British capitalism, supplying raw materials and buying manufactured goods. This policy was explicitly set out as the objective by the President of the Manchester Chamber of Commerce, Thomas Bazley, in his evidence to the 1840 parliamentary enquiry:

In India there is an immense extent of territory, and the population of it would consume British manufactures to a most enormous extent. The whole question with respect to our Indian trade is whether they can pay us, by the products of their soil, for what we are prepared to send out as manufactures.

The calculation here for the new stage of exploitation of India is as sharp and precise as the previous calculation of Clive three-quarters of a century earlier, already quoted, for the preceding stage.

To develop the Indian market it was necessary to develop the production and export of raw materials from India. It was to this objective that British policy now turned.

The importance of India to England in the first half of the century lay in the fact that India supplied some of the essential raw materials — hides, oil, dyes, jute and cotton — required for the industrial revolution in England, and at the same time afforded a growing market for English manufactures of iron and cotton. (*L. C. A. Knowles, "Economic Development of the Overseas Empire," p. 305.*)

The indication of the new stage of policy was the decision in 1833 to permit Englishmen to acquire land and set up as planters in India. In that same year slavery had been abolished in the West Indies. The new plantation system, which was nothing but thinly veiled slavery, was immediately developed in India, and it is significant that many of the original planters were slave drivers from the West Indies. ("Experienced planters were brought from the West Indies. . . . The area attracted a rather rough set of planters, some of whom had been slave drivers in America and carried unfortunate ideas and practices with them." Buchanan, "Development of Capitalist Enterprise in India," pp. 36–7.) The horrors that resulted were exposed in the Indigo Commission of 1860. To-day there are more than a million workers tied to the tea, rubber and coffee plantations, or more than the total number of workers in the textile, coal-mining, engineering, iron and steel industries combined.

The export of raw materials leapt up, especially after 1833. Raw cotton exports rose from 9 million pounds weight in 1813

to 32 million in 1833 and 88 million in 1844; sheep's wool from 3.7 thousand pounds weight in 1833 to 2.7 million in 1844; linseed from 2,100 bushels in 1833 to 237,000 in 1844. (Porter, "Progress of the Nation," 1847, p. 750.)

Between 1849 and 1914 exports of raw cotton rose from £1.7 million in value to £22 million. In weight, raw cotton exports rose from 32 million pounds in 1833 to 963 million in 1914, or thirty times over. Jute exports rose from £68,000 in 1849 to £8.6 million in 1914, or 126 times over.

Even more significant was the rising export of food grains from starving India. The export of food grains, principally rice and wheat, rose from £858,000 in 1849 to £3.8 million by 1858, £7.9 million by 1877, £9.3 million by 1901, and £19.3 million in 1914, or an increase twenty-two times over.

Alongside this process went a heavy increase in the number and intensity of famines in the second half of the nineteenth century. In the first half of the nineteenth century there were seven famines, with an estimated total of 1½ million deaths from famine. In the second half of the nineteenth century there were twenty-four famines (six between 1851 and 1875, and eighteen between 1876 and 1900), with an estimated total, according to official records, of over 20 million deaths. "Stated roughly, famines and scarcities have been four times as numerous during the last thirty years of the nineteenth century as they were one hundred years earlier, and four times more widespread" (W. Digby, "Prosperous British India," 1901). W. S. Lilley, in his "India and Its Problems," gives the following approximate figures on the basis of official estimates:

Years	Famine Deaths
1800–25	1,000,000
1825–50	400,000
1850–75	5,000,000
1875–1900	15,000,000

In 1878 a Famine Commission was appointed to consider the problem of the growing famines. Its Report, published in 1880, found that "a main cause of the disastrous consequences of Indian famines, and one of the greatest difficulties in the way of providing relief in an effectual shape is to be found in the fact that the great mass of the people directly depend on agriculture, and that there is no other industry from which any considerable part of the population derives its support."

At the root of much of the poverty of the people of India, and of the risks to which they are exposed in seasons of scarcity, lies the unfortunate circumstance that agriculture forms almost the sole occupation of the mass of the population, and that no remedy for present evils can be complete which does not include the introduction of a diversity of occupations, through which the surplus population may be drawn from agricultural pursuits and led to find the means of subsistence in manufactures or some such employments. (*Indian Famine Commission Report, 1880.*)

With these words Industrial Capital passed judgment on its own handiwork in India. . . .

The distinctive forms of nineteenth-century exploitation of India by industrial capital did not exclude the continuance of the old forms of direct plunder, which were also carried forward and at the same time transformed.

The "tribute," as it was still openly called by official spokesmen up to the middle of the nineteenth century, or direct annual removal of millions of pounds of wealth to England, both under the claim "home charges" as well as by private remitting, without return of goods to India (except for the proportionately small amount of governmental stores from England), continued and grew rapidly throughout the nineteenth century alongside the growth of trade. In the twentieth century it grew even more rapidly alongside a relative decline in trade.

In 1848, before the House of Commons Select Committee on Sugar and Coffee Planting in the West and East Indies, a Director of the East India Company, Colonel Sykes, estimated this "tribute," as he termed it, at £3½ million a year: "it is only by the excess of exports over imports that India can bear this tribute." Similarly N. Alexander, an East India merchant, reported to the same Committee: "Up to 1847 the imports of India were about £6,000,000, and the exports about £9,000,000. The difference is the tribute which the company received from the country, which amounts to about £4,000,000."

Between 1851 and 1901 the total remitted to England as "home charges" by the governing authority, excluding private remitting, multiplied sevenfold, from £2.5 million to £17.3 million, of which only £2 million represented purchases of stores. By 1913–14 it had risen to £19.4 million, of which only £1.5 million represented purchases of stores. By 1933–34 the net total of expenditure in England returned by the Government's accounts amounted to £27.5 million, of which only £1.5 million represented purchases of stores. . . .

The requirements of nineteenth-century free-trade capitalism compelled new developments of British policy in India.

First, it was necessary to abolish once and for all the Company and replace it by the direct administration of the British Government, representing the British capitalist class as a whole. This was partially realised with the new 1833 Charter, but only finally completed in 1858.

Second, it was necessary to open up India more completely for commercial penetration. This required the building of a network of railroads; the development of roads; the beginnings of attention to irrigation, which had been allowed to fall into complete neglect under British rule; the introduction of the electric telegraph, and the establishment of a uniform postal system; the first limited beginnings of an Anglicised education to secure a supply of clerks and subordinate agents; and the introduction of the European banking system.

All this meant that, after a century of neglect of the most elementary functions of government in Asia in respect of public works, the needs of exploitation now compelled a beginning to be made, although in an extremely one-sided and lop-sided fashion (while thwarting and strangling industrial development), directed only to meet the commercial and strategic needs of foreign penetration, and on extremely onerous financial terms to the people. . . .

But this process of active development, and especially of railway construction, necessitated by the requirements of industrial capital for the commercial penetration of India (as well as for a market for the iron, steel and engineering industries), carried with it an inevitable further consequence, which was to lay the foundations for a new stage — the development of British capital investments in India.

In the normal formula of imperialist expansion this process would be spoken of as the export of capital. But in the case of India, to describe what happened as the export of British capital to India would be too bitter a parody of the reality. The amount of actual export of capital was very small. Only over the seven years 1856–62 in the whole period up to 1914 was the normal excess of exports replaced by an excess of imports, totalling £22.5 million for the seven years — not a very large contribution for an ultimate total of capital investments estimated at close on £500 million by 1914. Over the period as a whole the export of capital from Britain to India was more than counterbalanced many times over by the contrary flow of tribute from India to England, even while the capital was being invested. *Thus the British capital invested in India was in reality first raised in India from the plunder of the Indian people, and then written down as debt owed by India to Britain, on which she had thenceforward to pay interest and dividends.*

The nucleus of British capital investments in India was the Public Debt — that favourite device already employed by the oligarchy in Britain to establish its stranglehold. When the British Government took over in 1858, they took over a debt of £70

million from the East India Company. In reality, as Indian writers have calculated, the East India Company had withdrawn in tribute from India over £150 million, in addition to the charges for the cost of wars waged by Britain outside India — in Afghanistan, China and other countries. On any correct drawing of accounts, there was thus a balance owing to India; but this naturally did not prevent the debt being taken over and rapidly increased.

In the hands of the British Government the Public Debt doubled in eighteen years from £70 million to £140 million. By 1900 it had reached £224 million. By 1913 it totalled £274 million. By 1939, on the eve of the Second World War, it totalled 11,790 million rupees (£884.2 million) divided into 7,099 million rupees (£532.4 million) of Indian debt and £351.8 million (4,691 million rupees) of sterling debt or debt in England. Thus in nearly three-quarters of a century of British direct rule the debt multiplied more than twelve times.

Especially significant was the growth of the proportion of the sterling debt in England. As late as 1856, at the end of the Company's rule, the debt in England was still under £4 million. By 1860 it had leapt to £30 million, by 1880 to £71 million, by 1900 to £133 million, by 1913 to £177 million, and by 1939 to £351.8 million.

The origin of this debt lay, in the first place, in the costs of wars and other charges debited to India, and later also in the costs of the railway and public works schemes initiated by the Government. The original £70 million had been largely built up by the wars of Lord Wellesley, the first Afghan Wars, the Sikh Wars and the suppression of the rising in 1857. Of the next £70 million, by which the British Government doubled the total in eighteen years, only £24 million were spent on State railways and irrigation works. Much of the rest of the debt was built up by the system of charging to India every conceivable charge that could be remotely or even fantastically connected with India and British rule in India. . . .

The burdens that it was found convenient to charge to India seem preposterous. The costs of the Mutiny, the price of the transfer of the Company's rights to the Crown, the expenses of simultaneous wars in China and Abyssinia, every governmental item in London that remotely related to India down to the fees of the charwomen in the India Office and the expenses of ships that sailed but did not participate in hostilities and the cost of Indian regiments for six months' training at home before they sailed — all were charged to the account of the unrepresented ryot. The Sultan of Turkey visited London in 1868 in state, and his official ball was arranged for at the India Office and the bill charged to India. A lunatic asylum in Ealing, gifts to members of a Zanzibar mission, the consular and diplomatic establishments of Great Britain in China and in Persia, part of the permanent expenses of the Mediterranean fleet and the entire cost of a line of telegraph from England to India had been charged before 1870 to the Indian Treasury. It is small wonder that the Indian revenues swelled from £33 million to £52 million a year during the first thirteen years of Crown administration, and that deficits accumulated from 1866 to 1870 amounting to £11½ million. A Home Debt of £30,000,000 was brought into existence between 1857 and 1860 and steadily added to, while British statesmen achieved reputations for economy and financial skill through the judicious manipulation of the Indian accounts. (*L. H. Jenks, "The Migration of British Capital," pp. 223–4.*)

The development of railway construction with State aid and guarantees for the private companies undertaking it, as well as later with direct State construction, enormously swelled the debt. The system adopted was one of a Government guarantee of 5 per cent interest for whatever capital was expended by British investors in the construction of the railways. It is evident that this system encouraged the most extravagant and uneconomic expenditure. The first 6,000 miles up to 1872 cost £100 million or over £16,000 a mile. "There was a kind of understanding," declared the former Government auditor of railway accounts to the Parliamentary Enquiry on Indian Finance in 1872, "that they were not to be controlled very closely . . . nothing was known of the money expended till the accounts were rendered." "Enormous sums were lavished," reported the former Finance Minister in India, W. N. Massey, to the same Enquiry, "and the contractors had no motive whatever for economy. All the money came from the English capitalist, and so long as he was guaranteed five per cent on the revenues of India, it was immaterial to him whether the funds that he lent were thrown into the Hooghly or converted into bricks and mortar. . . . It seems to me that they are the most extravagant works that were ever undertaken."

Up to the end of the nineteenth century £226 million were spent on railways, resulting, not in a profit, but in a loss of £40 million, which fell on the Indian Budget. After the turn of the century a profit was wrung out of the railways; and till 1943–4, when the sterling debt due to railways was repatriated, close on £10 million a year (£9.7 million in 1933–34) have been transmitted from India to England for railway debt.

With the development of railway construction, and also with the development of tea, coffee and rubber plantations and a few minor enterprises, private capital investment from Britain in India began to advance rapidly in the second half of the nineteenth century. . . .

For 1909–10 Sir George Paish, in a paper read before the Royal Statistical Society in 1911, estimated the total of British capital investments in India and Ceylon (excluding private capital other than of companies — i.e., capital for which no documentary evidence was readily available) at £365 million, composed as follows (*Journal of the Royal Statistical Society*, Vol. LXXIV, Part I, Jan. 2, 1911, p. 186):

Government and municipal	£182.5 million
Railways	136.5
Plantations (tea, coffee, rubber)	24.2
Tramways	4.1
Mines	3.5

Banks	3.4
Oil	3.2
Commercial and industrial	2.5
Finance, land and investment	1.8
Miscellaneous	3.3

It will be seen from this very instructive list that the process of British capitalist investment in India, or so-called "export of capital," did not by any means imply a development of modern industry in India. 97 per cent of the British capital invested in India before the war of 1914 was devoted to purposes of Government, transport, plantations and finance — that is to say, to purposes auxiliary to the commercial penetration of India, its exploitation as a source of raw materials and markets for British goods, and in no way connected with industrial development. . . .

The new basis of exploitation of India by British finance-capital, growing out of the conditions of the already existing industrial capitalist and trading exploitation of India, was from the outset, as the analysis by Sir George Paish of the composition of the capital invested in India by 1909–10 showed, auxiliary to the trading process and not replacing it. Nevertheless, a change in proportions developed of decisive significance for the modern era.

The British nineteenth-century industrial monopoly and domination of the world market began to weaken in the fourth quarter of the nineteenth century. In other parts of the world the decline before the new European and American rivals was marked. In India the decline was far slower, because the stranglehold was tenaciously held with the aid of political sovereignty. Even up to the war of 1914 Britain held fast nearly two-thirds of the Indian market against all the rest of the world. Yet also in India the decline slowly but steadily developed from the end of the third quarter of the nineteenth century.

In the five years 1874–79 the British share of Indian imports was 82 per cent, in addition to 11 per cent for the rest of the Empire, leaving less than one-fourteenth of the Indian market for the outside world.

By 1884–89 the British 82 per cent had fallen to 79 per cent. By 1899–1904 it had fallen to 66 per cent. By 1909–14 it had fallen to 63 per cent.

But at the same time the profits on invested capital and the volume of home charges were steadily rising. . . .

By 1914 the interest and profits on invested capital and direct tribute considerably exceeded the total of trading, manufacturing and shipping profits out of India. The finance-capitalist exploitation of India had become the dominant character in the twentieth century.

The war of 1914–18 and the subsequent period enormously accelerated this process. The British share of the Indian market fell from two-thirds to a little over one-third. Japanese, American and eventually renewed German competition pressed forward, despite tariffs and imperial preference. Indian industrial production made advances, principally in light industry, despite very considerable obstacles, financial difficulties and the deadweight of official discouragement, which was open in the pre-1914 period and continued in more veiled forms in the period following the war.

Between 1913 and 1931–32 the United Kingdom's share of Indian imports fell from 64 per cent to 35 per cent. . . .

But while the old basis was thus collapsing, the new basis of profits by finance-capitalist exploitation was steadily rising and extending in volume. By 1929 the total of British capital investments in India was estimated in the *Financial Times* by the former Secretary of the Bombay Chamber of Commerce, Mr. Sayer, at £573 million on the most conservative basis, and more probably £700 million. His calculation gave the following distribution:

Government Sterling Debt	£261 million
Guaranteed Railway Debt	120
5 per cent War Loan	17
Investments in Companies registered in India	75
Investments in Companies registered outside India	100

The figure of £175 million for companies operating in India was stated to be almost certainly an under-estimate, and a real total of £700 million for all investments "would probably not be very wide of the mark." He added:

The importance of our financial stake in India is fully recognized, probably, only by a limited number of experts. Most people have no real conception of either its magnitude or diversity. Many merchants, bankers and manufacturers who are actually engaged in the trade, would probably find it hard to arrive at even an approximate computation of the actual amount of the capital and services which is represented. External capital enters India in such a number of forms that any calculation must be largely guesswork. ("*Financial Times,*" *January 9, 1930.*)

A later estimate, for 1933, put forward by the British Associated Chambers of Commerce in India, made the total £1,000 million, represented by £379 million Government Sterling Debt, £500 million for companies registered outside India and operating in India, and the balance for investments in companies registered in India and miscellaneous investments.

This total of £1,000 million represented no less than one-quarter of the estimated total of £4,000 million of British foreign investments throughout the world. When Sir George Paish made his estimate in 1911, he found that British capital investments in India represented 11 per cent of the total of British capital investments throughout the world. *The advance from one-ninth to one-quarter, from 11 per cent to 25 per cent, is a measure of the increasing importance of India to British finance-capital in the modern period, and a key to modern imperialist policy with its special provisions for safeguarding British financial interests in India.*

What has been the value of the total tribute drawn from India to England each year by the modern imperialist methods of exploitation? An attempt to estimate this was made by the Indian economists, K. T. Shah and K. J. Khambata, in their "Wealth and Taxable Capacity of India," published in 1924. Basing their calculations on the available statistics for the year 1921–22 they reached the following result [of £146.5 millions]. . . .

The latest estimates of India's annual tribute to Britain have been given by Mr. Lawrence K. Rosinger, in his report, "Independence for Colonial Asia — the Cost to the Western World," issued by the Foreign Policy Association of America and published in 1945. According to him the annual tribute is £135 million comprised of items as below:

Interest charges on £670 million investments at British rate of interest 6–7–8 per cent	£46 million
Home Charges	33
Trade	30
Shipping	20
Remittances by Britishers serving in India	6
	£135 million

("*Hindustan Standard,*" *Calcutta, July 5, 1945.*)

After allowing the fullest margin of variation for the factors that cannot be exactly calculated, the broad conclusion is evident and inescapable that the exploitation of India in the modern period has been far more intensive than in the old. It was estimated that in the three-quarters of a century of British rule up to the taking over by the Crown, the total tribute withdrawn from India had amounted to £150 million. In the modern period, during the two decades before the war, it is estimated that the total *annual* tribute from India to England is in the neighbourhood of £135 million to £150 million. This intensified exploitation of India under the conditions of finance capitalism underlies the gathering crisis and intensified revolt against imperialism in India.

THE ECONOMIC IMPACT

The two readings in this section offer a more detailed examination of the impact of British rule on Indian economic life. The first excerpt, by Daniel Thorner (1915–　), focuses on the disintegration of the traditional village economy of rural India. Dr. Thorner, formerly on the faculty of the University of Pennsylvania, served from 1958 to 1960 in Bombay as Director, Census of India Research Project, Indian Statistical Institute. Since that time he has been *Directeur d'Études* in the *École Pratique des Hautes Études, Sixième Section, Sciences Économiques et Sociales,* at the Sorbonne in Paris. He is the author of numerous articles on Indian economic history, and has published three books, *Investment in Empire: The Founding of British Railway and Steam Shipping Enterprise in India, 1825–1849* (1950), *The Agrarian Prospect in India: Five Lectures on Land Reform* (1956), and, most recently, *Land and Labour in India* (1962).

The second selection, by Barbara Ward (1914–　), discusses some of the reasons why British rule brought only a limited degree of modernization to the Indian economy. Miss Ward, a member of the staff of *The Economist* of London since 1939, is widely known for her writings on world problems. She is the author of *Policy for the West* (1951), *The Interplay of East and West* (1957), *Five Ideas That Change the World* (1959), and *India and the West* (1961).

The Transformation of Rural Economy

DANIEL THORNER

THE development of the rural economy of India before independence may be divided into three periods: that of pre-British society (to 1793), the period in which new land systems were introduced (1793–1850), and that of the spread of commercial agriculture (1850–1947).

Pre-British Structure of Indian Society (to 1793). The outstanding feature of the economy of India before the advent of British power was the self-subsisting and self-perpetuating character of its typical unit, the village. India's villages functioned as little worlds of their own. The only outside authority which they acknowledged was that of some local princeling who in turn might be subordinate to a distant overlord.

The chief sign of submission to that authority was the payment of a share of the village crops.

Within the village social and economic relationships were governed by customary patterns and conventions of great antiquity. The cattle were tended and the soil was tilled by peasants whose fathers had been cultivators and whose sons would take their places when they came of age. Cloth for the garments of the peasants generally was spun and woven by families whose ancestors had been weavers long beyond the living memory of man. The other crafts were carried on by families which in effect were servants of the village. Their occupations passed on traditionally from father to son:

From the article by Daniel Thorner, "Economic Development — India before 1947," *The Encyclopedia Americana* (New York, 1960), XV, 12–14. By permission of *The Encyclopedia Americana*.

the blacksmith, potter, and carpenter, who made and repaired the implements and utensils of the village; the silversmith, who made the village jewelry; and the oilseed presser. For their services these craftsmen received a regular stipend from the crops of the villagers. In some areas hereditary servants and slaves attached to peasant households performed both domestic and agricultural duties.

The village itself consumed most of the raw materials it produced. Its needs for handicrafts were satisfied by the craftsmen associated with the village. It was this tight union of agriculture and hand industry which made the village independent of the outside world except for a few necessities like salt and iron. The share of the crops which went to the local magnate and moved on from him in a diminishing stream upward to the highest political overlord sustained the structure of government and provided subsistence for the urban population. As the local chiefs often constituted a rallying point against the center, some emperors and kings tried to weaken their power by collecting the land revenue without their participation. In their stead they created tax farmers or operated through subordinate revenue officials.

With the exception of pilgrimage centers, India's towns and cities generally were little more than headquarters for the top political overlords or imperial courts. The industries which were carried on in these cities were of two classes: those which met the minimum wants of the urban population, and those which provided mainly luxury goods for the upper classes or implements of war for the army. Economically, the cities had a one-way relation with the countryside, taking foodstuffs as tribute but supplying virtually no goods in return.

This was the structure of Indian society which the British found between 1750 and 1850 as they conquered one part of India after another. The basic land relationships were rooted in custom and usage rather than in statutes, legal cases, and court procedures. So long as the peasants turned over to the local potentate his customary tribute and rendered him the usual services, their right to till the soil and reap its fruits was taken for granted. Local rulers who repeatedly abused this right were considered oppressive; if they persisted, the peasants fled to areas where the customs of the land were better respected. As land was still available for settlement and labor was not too cheap, local chiefs had to be careful lest they alienate the villagers.

The British conquest of India through the agency of the East India Company led to the most drastic changes in the Indian way of life of which we have record. The most fundamental of these changes was the disintegration of the older structure of the village community, partly as a result of new land systems, and partly as a result of the spread of commercial agriculture.

Introduction of New Land Systems (1793–1850). In making arrangements for collecting land revenue in the areas of India which they conquered, the British were primarily concerned with securing the largest possible amount. For it was basically from these sums that British conquest and consolidation were financed. Two major types of land revenue systems were devised. In Bengal and adjacent areas, beginning in 1793, the British converted the tax farmers and revenue collectors into private landlords, granting them some of the rights of private property in the land. This was done on condition that the new landlords would raise greatly enhanced revenues from the cultivating peasants and pass the bulk of these revenues on to the state. This land revenue system is known as the zamindari system (from zamindar, or landholder).

An entirely different system was devised for large parts of Bombay and Madras and later applied to areas in the northeast and northwest. Here the British dealt directly with the individual peasants, for thereby they hoped to be able to obtain more revenue than under the zamindari system. Each peasant was recognized as holding the particular plot or plots he occupied, but his right to the land depended on annual payment in full of a heavy money rent to the government. Because it dealt directly with the peasant or ryot, the new system was called the ryotwari settlement. Whereas the zamindari system made the landlords masters of the village communities, the ryotwari system cut through the heart of the village communities by making separate arrangements between each peasant cultivator and the government.

These two systems were the dominant land systems of British India from 1793 to 1947. Under both of them the old body of custom was submerged by the formidable apparatus of law courts, fees, lawyers, and formal procedures. For with the introduction of some of the rights of private property in the land, the purchase and sale of zamindars' holdings were explicitly sanctioned by law. All of this was too much not only for the humble peasants, but also for the new landlords. Most of the latter could not raise the revenues required by the government and soon defaulted or sold out to merchants, speculators, and other sophisticated persons from the cities. The new landlords were interested only in the rents they could squeeze from the land; often they delegated the collection to middlemen who contracted to pay high sums annually. The latter sublet to other classes of middlemen, so that before long the unfortunate peasants of Bengal were supporting an impressive string of middlemen, speculators, and absentee landlords.

The ryotwari system also introduced some features of private property in land. The individual holders were registered and empowered to sell, lease, mortgage, or transfer their right to the use of the land. In contrast to the previous indigenous regimes, which had made more or less elastic demands, the British insisted on prompt payment of the stipulated sums. In cases of default livestock, household property, and personal effects might be attached, and the peasant might be evicted. The new system thus made mobile both the land and the peasant and left the way open for the growth in power of the moneylender and the absentee landlord.

Spread of Commercial Agriculture (1850–1947). The older rural framework of India, weakened by the new land systems, was shattered by the spread of commercial agriculture, the production of crops for sale rather than for family consumption. Commercial agriculture grew partly because of the recurring need of the peasants for money to meet the mounting demands made on them by the government and the landlords. Another reason was the fact that such a development was welcome to the British authorities. By the middle of the 19th century, Britain had passed through the Industrial Revolution. British industries were then the greatest in the world, and they kept on expanding. British manufacturers clamored for raw materials and sought good markets in which to dispose of their finished products. Under pressure from British merchants and manufacturers, India's coastal towns were linked with Britain in the 1840's by steamships, and the interior of India was covered after the 1850's by the most elaborate railway network in Asia.

Once the railways were opened, it became possible for the inland areas to produce for the world market. Wheat poured out of the Punjab, cotton out of Bombay, and jute out of Bengal. As commercial agriculture spread, the older practices associated with a self-subsisting economy declined. Since industrial crops (for example, cotton, peanuts, sugarcane, and tobacco) paid better than food grains, the peasants who could tended to shift over to them. In some districts the peasants shifted over completely to industrial crops and had to buy their foodstuffs from dealers. Villagers sent to market the cereal reserves traditionally kept for poor years. They became less prepared to meet poor harvests. Years of successive drought in the 1870's and 1890's led to great famines and agrarian unrest.

To produce crops for market the peasants required credit, and they turned to the moneylender, who came to occupy a place of unprecedented importance. Although in pre-British times the local moneylender extended casual credit to meet occasional needs, he occupied a subordinate place in the economy of the countryside. The new conditions, however, opened up a golden age for the moneylender. The demand for his services became an inescapable part of the peasant's life; to the government the moneylender was of invaluable aid in converting the peasant's crops into cash and passing on the land revenue. He was encouraged to expand his activities by the fact that he could now make a good and secure profit. If the peasants defaulted, he could use the new legal procedure to attach their lands, livestock, and personal possessions. Furthermore, from the middle of the 19th century the price of land rose rapidly, thereby encouraging the moneylender to broaden his operations. He began to take over the peasants' land and rent it out. The moneylenders grew in number and in wealth.

The same railroads which carried away the commercial crops brought back machine-made industrial products. The village artisans no longer were sheltered by the friendly backwardness of the older village commune, and the union of agriculture and hand industry which had been the basis of village life was disrupted. Under the impact of new forces the village could no longer remain a compact social and economic unit. The growing tendency was for each family to make ends meet as best it could. Deep in the interior of central India and in other areas difficult of access the handicrafts held on for a long time, but in the coastal zones and in the regions lying along the new railroads they declined. The village potter, tanner, dyer, oilman, and jeweler all faced strong competition from machine products.

Since 1850 a dwindling proportion of the village artisans have been able to subsist on what they have received for their services from the village. Millions of them have had to find other ways to gain a livelihood or to supplement their scanty earnings from the village. In most cases the only avenue open to them has been agriculture, and they have added steadily to the great pressure on the land.

The increase in the number of persons on the land did not reflect itself in an increase in production. Rather a number of related factors endemic in the rural situation served to hold agricultural output down. The hierarchy of rights in the land which was elaborated during the British period established more securely than ever before in Indian history the power of landholders to take a substantial share of the produce of the soil. Persons who enjoyed such rights tended to become set apart from those who actually tilled. Where owners and superior tenants subsisted primarily on rents, the portion remaining to inferior tenants and crop sharers was so small as to keep them stripped of capital; where hired laborers were employed, they were drawn typically from the lowest castes or tribes. Timorous, uneducated, ill paid, and with no stake in any increase in output, these laborers could hardly have been expected to take an interest in advanced techniques or even to make proper use of better tools. Crop production methods essentially remained the time-honored ones passed on from generation to generation.

Associated agrarian problems, such as insecurity of tenure, fragmentation of holdings, and concentration of credit and marketing in the hands of moneylenders, retarded productive investment in agriculture. Families with superior rights to sizable areas found it more remunerative to allow their holdings to be cultivated by others. Rather than plow back profits into the soil in order to obtain higher returns, they preferred to skim off as much rent as could be extracted on the basis of customary methods of production.

A formidable block against modernization was thus provided by a complex of factors which may be summed up in the expression "built-in depressor." Its effects may be seen in the fact that from 1890 to 1947 agricultural output rose so slowly that we are justified in speaking of stagnation. Whatever increases occurred in output took place in industrial crops; there are reasons for believing that to a significant extent these increases were achieved at the expense of food grains.

Modernization Begun but Not Completed

BARBARA WARD

BRITAIN's impact on the Indian economy illustrates in the clearest and most sustained way the general rule that, outside the Atlantic area, Western colonialism and Western investment launched but did not complete the processes of economic modernization; and if one reason more than any other is responsible for this phenomenon, it is that Western colonisers and Western investors throughout the crucial decades of predominant Western influence were mostly men who believed in *laissez faire*.

The system worked at home. By clearing away administrative obstructions, guaranteeing property and contract, and securing a general atmosphere of law and order, government had released an enormous flood of spontaneous economic energy which had transformed the old system with astonishing effectiveness and speed. Few people asked what might happen in a society in which the spontaneous energies were lacking — in which farmers worked only for subsistence, merchants and artisans had no sense of innovation, scientists and technicians were unknown, the leaders devoted themselves primarily to spending and display, and the whole ethics and purpose of the society were profoundly uncommercial. Such was India in the nineteenth century. It would have required heroic efforts comparable to the achievements of the Meiji reformers in Japan to have transformed the subcontinent into a modernized community. And the British could not be reformers on this scale.

For one thing, they were foreigners; and an alien government — unless it is a very ruthless one — tends to be cautious about root-and-branch reform. It may arouse more hostility than it can control. For another, the *laissez faire* of British officials in India must be considered rather an academic and specialized version of the faith. They had learned it at school and then carried it out to a vast pre-industrial economy where it was unlikely to be modified by the hard knocks of actual commercial experience. And they did not in any case feel much sympathy for whatever business groups there were, British or Indian. They had the instinctive prejudice against trade of Victorian gentlemen. They decidedly did not feel it the purpose of the British authorities in India to foster economic activities. Their task was to give law and order, administer justice, secure the land revenue, and give the mass of the people — overwhelmingly in the countryside — fair and consistent government. Where there was enterprise, such a system would not impede it and might even help — for instance, by securing internal peace, introducing modern commercial law, and ensuring orderly procedures in the courts. But where there was no enterprise,

Reprinted from *India and the West* by Barbara Ward, pp. 125–139. By permission of W. W. Norton & Company, Inc. Copyright © 1961 by W. W. Norton & Company, Inc. By permission also of Hamish Hamilton, Ltd., London.

government did not intend to act as a substitute.

A wholesale application of Britain's contemporary economic philosophy to the Indian world had the result of producing a system of partial modernization. On the land, it did begin to bring more farmers into the market. Partly this reflected the British decision to collect the land revenue in cash. The peasants had to sell to lay their hands on the money, and the impact was increased by the fact that, for some time, the level of assessment was on the whole too high. But the switch to the market also meant innovation and new methods for Indian farmers once internal peace and better communications began to widen the opportunities. Cash crops for export and for local industry or consumption expanded: jute around Calcutta, cotton and groundnuts in the enterprising Gujerat, wheat in the Punjab. By 1947 a considerable number of India's farmers had entered the market in one way or another. Even so, the majority still worked for subsistence.

Market influences were also extended — unconsciously — by the British in a different and less constructive sense. Applying British concepts of debt and property to Indian agriculture, they made land a salable commodity, which it had never been, allowed it to be mortgaged in return for credit, and permitted the courts to enforce foreclosure. The Indian peasant had always borrowed — to carry him over a poor harvest, to buy a new buffalo, to marry a daughter, to entertain his friends. But in the past the moneylender had no lien on his land, and by Hindu custom, interest payments beyond the sum of the principal went to reduce the debt. The situation could not get out of hand.

Under British administration, the peasant found he could borrow more than ever. The moneylenders had every inducement to stake him to the limit, knowing that the bondage of debt, thus established, would entail either the enslavement of the peasant who would now work the year round to pay interest on an accumulating debt, or else

the seizing of his land and its resale or reletting for a much higher return.

The pressures grew worse as the nineteenth century advanced. Decade after decade of internal peace brought a steady increase in India's population. There are no accurate statistics, but a rough estimate is that it may have doubled between 1780 and 1880. Thereafter it rose more rapidly — from over 200 millions in the last decades of the century to nearly 360 millions by the time of independence. More people in a still static economy meant more pressure on the land. Its market value rose, but the peasants grew poorer as their strips were subdivided. They fell more easily into debt and pledged their land more recklessly. And since its value was going up, creditors were readier to foreclose — while moneylenders, richer farmers, Zamindars were all drawn into the profitable but unproductive game of rural usury and land speculation.

The whole economy suffered as a result. Agricultural productivity did not improve, and there was no growing surplus of food to transfer to urban markets. Although landlords could make large gains by usury and by speculating in land, they had little inducement to use their money for improving their farms. Nor had the wretched peasant any inducement to do so. Any surplus he might have earned by producing more efficiently for the market would have been instantly drained off to the *bania* — the moneylender — either in the shape of compound interest on past debts or else by way of current market transactions. The *banias* were usually merchants as well, buying the peasants' produce at low prices just after the harvest, since the little men could not afford to wait, and then selling him back his seed corn, his implements, and his domestic necessities at whatever price the market would bear. Between his low selling price and his high buying price the peasant's surplus vanished. This left him with no spur to greater efficiency.

Wherever such a type of self-perpetuating rural stagnation has appeared — in Japan before 1868, in China before 1949, in the latifundia of Southern Europe, or the feudal systems of Latin America — it has proved a source of dangerous immobility to the whole economy and hence a potent spur to revolutionary discontent. . . .

To begin to break away from this type of self-perpetuating and disintegrating stagnation, there is only one sure way — decisive land reform; and whenever it has not been attempted, the prospects for either economic progress or democratic institutions must be judged very bleak. But as an alien power the British Government could not adopt such a solution in India. And its failure on the land impeded efforts of modernization in other sectors. The essence of a successful breakthrough to economic growth is that its effects should be cumulative — each sector providing stimulus to the rest, and the expansion of a growing number of concurrent activities providing external economies, markets, supplies, and opportunities to each dynamic element in the new economy. Partial modernization changes and develops sections of the economy, provides spurts of energy and growth, and increases some incomes and opportunities — but the cumulative effect is lacking. This was the pattern in British India.

In two vital sectors of the economy — the provision of the system's infrastructure of transport, power, education, and so forth, and in manufacturing — the failure of modernization in agriculture helped to keep development below the level needed for self-sustaining growth. Even if government had been less wedded to *laissez faire,* it would still have been limited in its activities by its continuing poverty. Land revenue was one of its chief sources of income, but stagnant agriculture prevented any important increase. As for the industrial sector, the rural blight impeded its growth by drawing off potential investment into usury and land speculation and by keeping peasant consumption below the level at which the villages might have become effective markets for an industrial sector producing consumer goods.

Actually the Indian government did

break some new ground in the sphere of infrastructure. In nineteenth-century Britain, the economy's overheads had been largely provided by private enterprise. The greatest single element — the railways — had been built by private capital, not only in Britain but, with the help of British investment, all around the Atlantic world as well. Even education, which governments everywhere have accepted as their responsibility, was largely privately provided in Britain until the last decades of the century. In India, in spite of the prevailing philosophy of nonintervention, government did stimulate some elements of infrastructure. It was clear that private initiative would not produce even the beginnings of a modern system of education, so this the government set out to do, concentrating, as in England, on the training of an elite at the secondary and university level. And the Indian railways were also financed on government initiative and with government guarantees, which enabled the money to be raised relatively inexpensively. In 1914, India, with 40,000 miles of track, had one of the largest systems in the world. Its principal purpose had been, in the government's eyes, to ensure Indian security — internally against the risk of disaffection, externally against possible encroachment. But its economic effect was immediate and widespread. It broke down provincial isolation and permitted the administration, after some disastrous efforts to leave the matter to the workings of the market, to evolve a proper famine code and deal effectively with the recurring crisis of failure of the monsoons. Above all, the railway system began to create a unified internal market and to stimulate the more vigorous and enterprising regions — the Punjab, Gujerat — to produce for it.

But at this point the record of the government's direct stimulus more or less ends. Nor did it try indirectly to promote growth by a better mobilization of private capital. Most banks were foreign and concerned in the main with foreign trade. Indian banking was not far removed from old-fashioned

money lending. The stock exchanges in
Bombay and Calcutta served a very restricted group. There was no central bank
until the 1920s. Thus, even if more Indians had been interested in investment —
and most were not — they would have
found it hard to find the right channels.
The government's attitude to the unorgan-
ized capital market was, of course, entirely
in keeping with *laissez faire*. In Britain,
private enterprise had created its own credit
institutions. In India, the underlying enterprise was lacking, and so the system failed
to take root. There was no attempt made to
follow the precedent of the railways and
build up by government stimulus what private enterprise could not produce itself.

Even the interventions that were made
had less than their full possible effect. All
the equipment for the railways was bought
in Britain, and provided no stimulus to
local industrialization beyond a few railway
workshops — and even then the engineers
were mainly British. Another potent public spur to industrial growth — a defence
establishment and an arms industry — also
failed to develop. After the Mutiny, only
small arms were manufactured in India.
Artillery, an important element in the expansion of heavy industry, was procured
from Britain. India's few ordnance establishments remained too small to boost local
engineering. Shipbuilding, which the Japanese government encouraged with considerable effect in the early stages of growth,
was not carried on in India at all, a consequence of the Westerners' early capture of
seaborne traffic and Britain's later engross-
ment of the Indian carrying trade. Thus
India missed two or three of the main nineteenth-century boosts to growth.

These lacks should not be laid to some
special and devious British desire to stunt
Indian development. At that time, no one
knew how vast were India's reserves of iron
ore — some twenty billion tons — for the de-
posits lay out in the jungles of Bihar and
Orissa. The raw materials for iron and steel
making were not ready to hand, as they had
been in Britain and America or Germany

or Lorraine. Thus it seemed cheaper and
more sensible to go shopping for industrial
and military supplies in the developed
West. However, a government really set
on modernizing the economy might have
done more. Japan, too, lacked iron ore and
coking coal in the 1870s. But the Meiji
reformers began to build up an arms industry all the same.

And, having missed some of the central
nineteenth-century accelerators, India proceeded to miss the twentieth-century types
as well. Roads remained inadequate and in
large parts of the country quite primitive.
There was no large development of electric
power. Coal production, having risen from
a million tons to 20 million tons a year between 1880 and the First World War, rose
little further. Technical and scientific education — the essential modern pendants to
the old classical training — expanded hardly
at all. At independence, the number of
students graduating in engineering and
technology was still only about 3,000 a year.

The truth is, that in the interwar years,
Britain was no longer in a position to keep
up the tempo of earlier development. The
twenties and the thirties brought stagnation
to the British economy and there was no
capital to spare for the colonies. And in
India the steadily growing pressure of nationalist opposition to British rule absorbed
the administration's funds and attention to
the exclusion of nearly everything else. As
a result, the few modest signs in the twenties and thirties of a new governmental
approach — the departments to encourage
industrial development, the new interest in
agricultural extension work and research —
never really got under way for lack of
funds. In 1939, India was still essentially
an economy with a nineteenth-century, not
a twentieth-century framework.

In these conditions of relative stagnation,
private enterprise alone could not act as a
spur to sustained growth. For many years
the chief investments were, inevitably, British, but they never reached a level sufficient
to launch a general expansion. Before the
first World War, all Britain's investments,

public and private, in India amounted to not much more than 16 per cent of British overseas investment, the bulk of which had gone to the temperate lands. At independence, private investment stood at $423 millions and had been at about that level for the thirty preceding years. Thus, after more than a century of its connection with India, Britain's total private capital there was considerably less than the figure for today's capital exports in a single year.

The most usual criticism today is not, however, that foreign investment in developing countries remains too small, but that it tends to engross too large a share of the country's resources and opportunities. Why, so run the arguments, permit foreign capital to come in and develop a concession when the result is that the entire earnings are shipped overseas as payments to shareholders and creditors, as disbursements for royalties and patents, and as salaries and pensions to foreign executive and technical staff? All that remains in the host country is a small sum for wages — which will be low because workers can still be hired for subsistence pay — and perhaps some money spent on local supplies — unless all these, too, are shipped in from abroad. In these conditions the enterprise to all intents and purposes is not in the local economy at all. If, in addition, it is developing a wasting asset — a gold reef or a copper mine — the final result will be to lose the asset and gain nothing in return. Or if the goods the company manufactures are sold locally and earn no foreign exchange, the need to repay profits and repatriate capital in foreign currency may greatly add to the problems of the country's balance of payments.

Where these conditions prevail, foreign investment clearly contributes very little to local expansion; and all around the world there are static subsistence economies coexisting with pockets of advanced technology and production run by foreigners developing resources solely for the foreign user and contributing very little to local dynamism. The cultivation system in the Dutch East Indies was an instance of this,

or the early stages of rice development in Lower Burma during which the entire surplus went to British or Indian middlemen. The local peoples are not necessarily worse off — though the Javanese finally were — but they are not drawn into the functions or the rewards of new economy. Like children with their noses against the shop window, they see the sweets but they cannot go in and buy. This frustrating "demonstration effect" is, like the agrarian stagnation which often accompanies it, fine ammunition for Communist propaganda.

Few of Britain's investments in India fitted into these extreme categories. Many of the export crops — especially tea and jute — became handsome earners of foreign exchange. Between 1868 and 1928, India's exports quintupled and its imports increased eightfold. This represents a sizable contribution to national income; and since some of the crops stimulated or expanded by British enterprise — cotton, jute, groundnuts, pepper — were grown by local farmers, gains from the export trade contributed directly to their income. Around Bombay, there were even signs of a wider economic acceleration in the second half of the nineteenth century; and after 1886, when general income taxes had been introduced, earnings from foreign enterprise began to make some direct contribution to local revenue.

Admittedly more of the surplus would have remained in India if all enterprise had been Indian. But in the conditions prevailing in the early nineteenth century, this is precisely what could not happen without a jolt from outside. There were no Westernizing influences at work in India, studying and judging Western growth as the Rangakusha scholars had done in eighteenth-century Japan or the "Western Group" of Takashima and Noboru a century later. There were no influential modernizers, no prince with the enterprise of a Peter the Great to go off and learn at first hand the facts about Western development. Before the British came to demonstrate what a modern enterprise looked like, there were no indigenous patterns. Even the cloth trade of Bengal, which in the late eighteenth century exported as much as £3 millions' worth of goods to Britain in a single year, was organized by the factors of the East India Company, who harried the weavers and brought back the cloth. It is sometimes argued that if cheap textiles from Lancashire had not wiped out this export, it might have become the nucleus of a purely Indian development. But it was factory competition that destroyed the old handicraft exports; and to compete with manufactured textiles, Bengal enterprise would have needed speedy access to modern forms of power. In Lancashire, coal and the steam engine preceded the revolution in textiles. But the first Indian coal was not mined until the jute interests opened up the Raniganj colliery in 1854. What was lacking around Calcutta half a century sooner was that confluence of a wide variety of different techniques, discoveries, enterprises, and investments — of which textiles were only one — which had launched Britain on its revolution.

In the conditions of the early nineteenth century, British capital and skill brought in from outside were not ousting local efforts. On the contrary, they were needed to stimulate, at some point, effective local imitation. Once the railways were built, and peace, order, and dependable law had become habitual, Indian business did appear. Where enterprise was strong, chiefly in the Gujarat areas around Bombay, local cotton merchants, many of them Parsees, established a large modern textile industry on the basis of indigenous cotton. The most successful of them, the Tata family, went on to launch other ventures, including the first Indian steel industry, just before the First World War — even though, to do this, the firm had to accomplish a pioneering job at Jamshedpur, hacking the enterprise out of virgin jungle and opening up access for the first time to India's vast reserves of iron ore.

However, in spite of this growth of Indian enterprise, British interests remained strongly entrenched. Much of what was Indian business in capital and control was nevertheless managed by British firms. The system of managing agents by which a company, in return for a fee or a percentage of the profits, provided management for other enterprises, supplemented the shortage of Indian managers and was a convenience to British investors who wanted to invest their money in India but did not want to live there to supervise it themselves. Inevitably, as the sense of India's separate political destiny increased, the extent of British control and interest in Indian business began to be resented. There were more Indians now who felt they could take the British place. What had been a spur was felt to be growing into something of an incubus. And resentment was sharpened by the memory of some elements of real discrimination.

In the main, it could be said that the British authorities had not practised discrimination against Indian enterprise. They had simply failed to help everybody. But in one local application of the rules of *laissez faire*, it must be allowed that British policy loaded the scales in Britain's favour and made a marked — and avoidable — contribution to the relative sluggishness of industrial growth in India. The Indian government was allowed to introduce tariff protection only after 1919. As a result, throughout the fifty years before the First World War, Indian enterprise always had to compete against experienced, established British firms whose products were cheaper and better known than anything a local industry could produce in its first experimental stages. That this had an inhibiting effect is confirmed by the country's experience after 1919. Between the wars, in spite of the general stagnation of the world economy, Indian enterprise managed to launch out into new lines — sugar, cement, paper — even though the procedures for procuring tariff protection were stiff and cumbersome. It is impossible to doubt that similar protection earlier would have given Indian industry a larger base. In particular, the Indian textile industry must have captured more of the internal market. But here, the interests of British industry were allowed to predominate. In fact, when for a time the Government in India put a small revenue tariff on imported textiles, pressure in Britain succeeded in adding an equivalent levy on local cloth. The rationale might be argued to be one of pure free trade. The effect was protection for Lancashire.

In 1939, after a hundred years of British investment, peace, order, and modern commercial law, after nearly a century of modern railways, ports, and exports industries, after eighty years of Indian enterprise in a vast internal market of 300 million souls, India still had an industrial establishment of only 2 million workers, a steel output of less than a million tons, and a population which still depended for as much as 80 per cent of its livelihood on a static, overcrowded, agrarian economy. Not by any stretch of the imagination can this be called a record of dynamic growth. It is simply the first sketch of a first beginning. It was not therefore surprising that when the Indians achieved independence, they had one purpose above all others — to reorder their economy and catch up with the long arrears of stagnation and lost opportunity. And if there is a single definition to cover the aims of the economic plans which have since been carried through, it is to bring the Indian economy fully into the twentieth century and carry through the changes in agriculture, in infrastructure, in industrial development without which it can have no hope of achieving the dynamism of sustained growth.

THE POLITICAL ASPECT (I)

No discussion of the spirit or structure of Britain's government in India can be purely academic in nature. Inevitably it must reflect one's view of the legitimacy of British control and of the legitimacy of nationalist demands. The excerpts which follow have been chosen to illustrate the contrast in outlook which prevailed in the early 1940's, only a few years before British rule came to an end. Particular attention should be paid to the divergent interpretations of the Government of India Act of 1935.

The first reading is from a volume published in 1941 under the auspices of the Royal Institute of International Affairs. L. S. S. O'Malley (1874–1941), the author of the first selection, served as a member of the Indian Civil Service from 1898 to 1924. He was the author of *The Indian Civil Service, 1601–1930* (1931), *Indian Caste Customs* (1932), *India's Social Heritage* (1934), and *Popular Hinduism* (1935), as well as editor and part author of *Modern India and the West: A Study in the Interaction of Their Civilizations* (1941), from which this reading is taken.

Kate L. Mitchell (1909–), an American author, had been a member of the secretariat of the Institute of Pacific Relations for almost a decade when she wrote *India without Fable* in 1942. Her other books include *Japan's Industrial Strength* (1942) and *The Industrialization of the Western Pacific* (1942).

British Rule and Indian Welfare

L. S. S. O'MALLEY

A RESOLUTION passed by the House of Commons in 1793 affirmed that it was the peculiar and bounden duty of the legislature to promote by all just and prudent means the interest and happiness of the British dominions in the East. It was thus recognized that, in the words used by Lord William Bentinck in 1804, the system was to be one which founded British greatness on Indian happiness. This necessarily involved the establishment of law and order, the administration of even-handed justice, the maintenance of public, and the protection of private, rights — in other words, the discharge of the primary functions of government as understood in the West. India, however, was not a *tabula rasa*. It was a land with well-established social and legal institutions, and the question arose whether and to what extent the system of government should follow Indian or European models and whether pre-existing institutions should be retained or should be discarded in favour of importations from the West. Questions of both principle and policy were involved. How far could the *status quo* be maintained without sacrifice of the moral and political principles of the

From the section by L. S. S. O'Malley, in L. S. S. O'Malley (ed.), *Modern India and the West: A Study in the Interaction of Their Civilizations* (London, 1941), pp. 98–100, 587–589, 594–601, published by the Oxford University Press under the auspices of the Royal Institute of International Affairs. By permission. (In one instance the excerpts have been rearranged from their order of appearance in the original work.)

British and without injury to their convictions of what was right? How far could administration be westernized without causing dislocation which might do more harm than good? Was, in fact, any synthesis possible between the static ideas of the East and the progressive ideas of the West? The position of the British, faced with this dilemma, has aptly been compared with that of men forced to make their watches keep time in two longitudes, neither too fast to endanger security nor too slow to impede progress. In the end there was the usual British solution of the problem — a kind of compromise — but on the whole the tendency was to westernization, the dominant principle being that expressed by Lord Lawrence: "In doing the best we can for the people, we are bound by our conscience and not by theirs."

In the early days of their dominion the British endeavoured to build on the foundations already laid, though the actual superstructure of government had collapsed. It was one of Warren Hastings's cardinal principles that the government, while discharging its responsibility as the guardian of civil rights, should, as far as possible, maintain Indian institutions. As he himself declared, his object was to establish a system which would possess an authority founded on the ancient laws of India, and which would enable the people to be ruled with ease and moderation according to their own ideas, manners, and prejudices.

In a word, let this be the working principle of our government of the people, whose ease and welfare we are bound both by justice and policy to preserve: to make their laws sit as light on them as possible and to share with them the principles of our own constitution where they are capable of partaking of them consistently with their other rights and the welfare of the state.

Accordingly, the ancient landmarks were not removed. The Hindu and Islamic systems of personal law were maintained, the Islamic penal law continued to be adminis-

tered, Indian personnel was employed in the administration, and the executive system followed the lines already laid down by the Mughals, i.e., there was a chain of officials, each with jurisdiction over a definite area, through whom the orders of the government were transmitted and by whom they were executed. An Anglicizing tendency set in under Lord Cornwallis, who excluded Indians from offices of trust and responsibility, remoulded the administration more in consonance with European ideas, and revolutionized the agrarian system in Bengal, Bihar, and some adjoining areas by means of the Permanent Settlement, which introduced an English form of landed property. Landholders who had been liable to displacement by the State acquired a status resembling that of English landlords, being made owners of the soil not in recognition of any pre-existing right, but as a measure of policy dictated by English ideas of the value of a squirearchy. The Anglicizing tendency was checked in 1833, when a parliamentary committee, which held the usual inquiry into the administration of India before the renewal of the charter of the East India Company, laid down that the laws of India should be adapted to the feelings and habits of Indians rather than to those of Europeans, condemned the racial discrimination which had resulted in the exclusion of Indians from all but subordinate posts, and declared that it was recognized that the interests of Indian subjects should be consulted in preference to those of Europeans whenever the two came into conflict. This declaration, which was inspired by the humanitarian ideas derived largely from the evangelical movement in England, was a remarkable advance in the conception of the relations between a European nation and one of its dependencies. It had been the general belief that the interests of the latter should be subordinated to those of the former, and it was now enunciated as a guiding principle that the welfare of the subject race should have priority over the advantage of the ruling race, though it must be added that this principle was not always honoured in practice.

The Charter Act of 1833 specifically provided that no Indian should be debarred from holding any office by reason only of his religion, place of birth, descent, or colour. The Board of Directors followed this up with a dispatch pointing out that it meant that in future there should be "no governing caste" in British India and that Indians were to be admitted to places of trust as freely and fully as regard to the due discharge of the functions attached to them would allow. In other words, capacity and not race was to be the criterion of eligibility for administrative offices. Indians were accordingly appointed in increasing numbers to responsible judicial and executive posts, but not to the *corps d'élite* represented by the Indian Civil Service, which had a monopoly of the higher posts. There was moreover no idea of associating Indians with the government as distinct from the administration of the country. Representative institutions were regarded as absolutely out of the question; no one, however democratic his views, suggested their introduction. In the House of Commons debate on the Act of 1833 Lord Macaulay envisaged the possibility that by means of good government India might be educated into a capacity for better government and might in some future age demand European institutions, but such a prospect was admittedly visionary.

In India [he said] you cannot have representative institutions. . . . We have to frame a good government for a country into which, by universal acknowledgement, we cannot introduce those institutions which all our habits, which all the reasonings of European philosophers, which all the history of our own part of the world lead us to consider as the one great security for good government.

*   *   *

In the second half of the nineteenth century the pendulum swung in the direction of greater westernization of the system of government. There was a demand for more precise methods of administration and for an extension of the range of governmental functions, as the result of the pressure partly of public opinion in Great Britain and partly of educated opinion in India, which became more exacting in its requirements. As the government became more closely organized and its functions were enlarged, the services of professional administrators became more necessary, and it became more of a government by experts, Indian as well as British, who were exempt from interference by popularly constituted bodies. It was from this time that the administration began to be called bureaucratic. The term was correct in one sense, inasmuch as the work of government was in the hands of governors by profession, which as J. S. Mill said, is the essence and meaning of bureaucracy. It also connotes, however, government by and from offices, whose chief task is to make and enforce rules and regulations, and from this point of view it was not altogether applicable.[1] The system in India was not one of mere office control. There were secretariats and various departments for special branches of administration, such as excise, education, forests, public works, and jails; there were rules and regulations galore; but the basis of the administration, the essential feature which differentiated it from an impersonal bureaucracy of the western kind, was the district officer, in whom local authority was concentrated and who was peripatetic for a considerable part of the year, moving from place to place, in touch with all classes, investigating local conditions, inquiring into complaints, redressing, if possible, grievances on the spot, and, in general, giving the people a form of personal rule.

[1] The commentary of Sir Henry Maine is of interest. "The dyslogistic language now coming into use imputes nothing but knowledge and experience. The Indian bureaucracy is merely a barbarous foreign phrase applied with gross inaccuracy to as remarkable a body of public servants as any country has produced, engaged in administrating the affairs of a vast population under perfectly definite and intelligently stated rules." T. H. Ward, *The Reign of Queen Victoria* (1887), p. 524.

His name and fame live after him, if only he is left long enough in a district to make an impress on it, whereas the memory of the secretariat officer is soon lost in oblivion.

The range of State activities was steadily extended, English law was made the basis of codes which followed in quick succession, and the influence of English principles and practice was seen in the general administration. Sir Fitzjames Stephen, who, as Law Member of Council from 1869 to 1872, had an important part in the codification of the law, expressed the opinion that the Mutiny was in its essence a breakdown of an old system, the renunciation of an attempt to effect an impossible compromise between the Asiatic and the European view of things, legal, military, and administrative. The compromise might not have been impossible, but the Mutiny left British officials with little stomach for compromise and with feelings of bitterness against oriental methods. The old idea of governing the people in their own way had been so disastrous in its results that the government must now do what it considered best for them, whether to their liking or not.

The government was, as Lord Lawrence pointed out in 1858, a trustee for the people, but not in the sense that it was bound by the will of the people. "We have not been elected or placed in power by the people, but we are here through our moral superiority, by the force of circumstances, by the will of Providence. This alone constitutes our charter to govern India." The criterion of public good was not the popular will but the ruling power's ideas of duty and obligation, and it held itself bound to do good to the people according to its own light and not theirs. The idea of trusteeship in the sense of tutelage as a training for self-government was at the same time not forgotten in spite of the revulsion of feeling caused by the Mutiny. There were men like Sir Herbert Edwardes who could declare publicly that England should set before her the policy of first fitting India for freedom and then setting her free. England, which at the time (1860) was

shouting across the narrow seas "Italy for the Italians," would in time, he hoped, lift its voice still higher and shout across the world "India for the Indians." It might take years — even a century — to fit India for self-government, but it was a thing worth doing and a thing that might be done. England might then gladly and proudly leave India, the stately daughter she had reared, to walk the future with a free imperial step, with her resources developed and her people enlightened, awakened, and no longer isolated in the East but linked with the civilized races of the West. He himself contemplated an India no longer idolatrous or caste-ridden, but converted to, and regenerated by, Christianity, and he held that till she was leavened with Christianity she would be unfit for freedom; but others took a more secular view and did not postulate christianization as a qualification for self-government.

It has been said by a wise Indian administrator that what the masses desire above all things is to be left alone, but it is the misfortune of the mission of England that it cannot leave them alone. Actually its mission was to give India the best form of government that it was capable of giving and India was capable of receiving, and if this task was to be accomplished, the *status quo* had to be disturbed. Specialized departments of government were created which affected the individual and the public in many different ways. The preservation of indigenous forms of organization was no longer a primary consideration; the spirit of individualism, so congenial to the British temperament, led to the recognition of the individual in place of collective responsibility. The watchword was progress and reform, and the semi-communal village life, which, it must be admitted, was largely static, was regarded as unequal to the requirements of a progressive administration. In order therefore to attain efficiency, work which had been done by the cooperative efforts of villagers was brought under control or handed over to agents responsible to the government and not to the village community. This general statement of the trend of administration is, however, subject to considerable qualification. The country being too poor to bear the expense of the machinery of a modern European State, considerations of economy limited the strength of the administrative staff and circumscribed the circle of its activities. The State was not a Leviathan, and there was nothing like regimentation. . . .

The cult of efficiency was followed without any doubts as to its virtue till well into the twentieth century, and its high priest was Lord Curzon [Viceroy, 1899–1905]. "Efficiency," he declared, "has been our gospel, the key-note of our administration." His justification of his creed should at the same time be quoted. "Efficiency of administration is, in my view, a synonym for the contentment of the governed. It is the one means of affecting the people in their homes and of adding only an atom it may be, but still an atom, to the happiness of the people." Like many other Victorians, he held that national prosperity lay in their material well-being. This was the *summum bonum*, all that India in the stage she had reached either needed or could desire. He conscientiously and steadfastly believed that the good of India would be secured not by self-government but by good government; and good government must be of the British pattern and no other. "We have come here with a civilization, an education, and a morality which we are vain enough, without disparagement to others, to think the best that have ever been seen, and we have been placed, by the Power that ordains all, in the seats of the mighty." The rule of India being a British rule, and any other rule being in the circumstances of the case impossible, the tone and standard should be set by those who had created it and were responsible for it. By virtue of their upbringing, education, and knowledge of the principles of government, Englishmen possessed the habits of mind and vigour of character essential for the task. Consequently, the highest posts of civil employment, i.e., those in the Indian Civil Service, though open to Indians, should as a general rule be held by Englishmen. Outside this *corps d'élite,* however, the policy was to restrict rather than extend European agency and to enlist Indians as fully as possible in the service of the State; and Lord Curzon had good reason for claiming that its result had been to establish a European system of government entrusted largely to non-European hands. He looked forward to the time when India would be raised from the level of a dependency to the position which was bound to be hers, if it was not hers already, that of the greatest partner in the Empire, but her advance was to be by means of paternal government under British control. Government was and should remain, a benevolent despotism; if it sacrificed its despotism, it would sacrifice its benevolence. In 1900 he expressed the belief that the Congress was tottering to its fall and said that one of his great ambitions was to assist it to a peaceful demise. A little over three years later he admitted that public opinion was daily becoming more powerful; but at the end of his term of office he briefly dismissed the idea of political advance with the remark that he had not offered political concessions because he did not regard it as wisdom or statesmanship in the interests of India to do so. It can scarcely be doubted that he overlooked or under-estimated the strength of the forces which were at work.

There had already been some political progress. One result of the increasingly close nexus of administration was to create conditions with which a system of autocracy, however benevolent, was incompatible. So long as the people were left largely to themselves, such a system could be maintained, but the more detailed regulation of their affairs made it desirable that they should be consulted and given a voice in their government. This principle was recognized by the constitution of Legislative Councils in 1861, and more fully by the Indian Councils Act of 1892, which widened the basis of government by giving further opportunities to non-official Indian elements to take part in its work. A step in the direction of autonomy in local affairs was also taken in 1870, when Lord Mayo's government issued a resolution acknowledging the need of local interest and supervision for the management of funds devoted to education, sanitation, medical relief, and local public works. With this object a system of local self-government was to be developed and municipal institutions were to be strengthened. This was followed by a series of legislative enactments, which established a system of local bodies organized not on Indian but on British lines, and which gave partial effect to the elective principle.

The change which had by this time come over the conception of the problem of government cannot be better illustrated than by the remarks made in 1878 by the Viceroy, Lord Lytton, with which may be compared the views already quoted, which had been expressed by Warren Hastings about a century before.

The problem undertaken by the British rulers of India (a political problem more perplexing in its conditions and, as regards the result of its solution, more far-reaching than any which, since the dissolution of the Pax Romana, has been undertaken by a conquering race) is the application of the most refined principles of European government and some of the most artificial institutions of European society to a vast Oriental population, in whose history, habits, and traditions they have had no previous existence. . . .

After referring to the fact that to the vast mass of the people British rule appeared to be a foreign, and more or less uncongenial system of administration, which was scarcely, if at all, intelligible to the greater number of those for whose benefit it was maintained, he went on to say:

It is a fact which there is no disguising, and it is also one which cannot be too constantly or too anxiously recognized, that by enforcing these principles and establishing these institutions we have placed and must permanently maintain ourselves at the head of a gradual

but gigantic revolution — the greatest and most momentous social, moral, and religious, as well as political, revolution which perhaps the world has ever witnessed.

This diagnosis of the processes in operation is remarkable for its insight and is of more than temporary or transitory interest, indicating, as it does, the lines which were now being consciously followed.

A lesson learnt by the British from their own history is that a constitution should be a growth, not a creation *per saltum*. They were therefore chary of making new constitutions for India, "as though," to quote Arthur Young's remark about the French, "constitutions were a pudding to be made from a recipe." Three new constitutions however have been inaugurated within the last thirty-one years, each more liberal than the last. The first, which came into force in 1909, was an attempt to blend principles of autocracy inherited from Hindu kings and Mughal emperors with principles of democracy derived from Great Britain. In 1917 the British government announced that its policy was the gradual development of self-governing institutions with a view to the progressive realization of responsible government in India as an integral part of the British Empire. This definitely marked the parting of the ways. Absolute government was to be discarded; responsible government by the people themselves was to come ultimately, although there was as yet no popular demand for it. There was a demand from an educated minority, but the great majority had as yet neither the desire nor the capacity for it. It was, however, felt by the British government that a beginning could and should be made for the sake of the national life of India. The people should not be dependent on a paternal government but learn to stand on their own feet. For this purpose the forms of government which had grown up on British soil were to be transplanted to a country with a long tradition of autocracy. "We believe," wrote the authors of the scheme, "that the placid, pathetic contentment of the masses is not the soil on which Indian nationhood will grow and that, in deliberately disturbing it, we are working for her highest good." "Our reason is the faith that is in us";[2] and that faith was western in conception.

Nationalism, striving to develop a sense of nationhood, grew apace during the next decade (1921–31). Political consciousness increased, and, alien though they were, the principles and practices of the British parliamentary system were accepted as the norm. Finally, in 1931, the British government announced its determination that the responsibility for the government of British India should be transferred from the British parliament to Indian legislatures (central and provincial). There was to be a democratic government of the English pattern, with an executive responsible to a popular assembly, the members of which in their turn were to be responsible to an electorate — in other words, a parliamentary system modelled on that of Great Britain. Six years later a reformed constitution came into effect, by which a decisive voice in the civil administration of the different provinces has been given to elected representatives, while provision is made for the creation of an all-Indian federation combining British India and the States in a political unity, with representatives of the electoral system of British India and representatives of the personal rule of the Indian States forming a unified government.

* * *

The fruition of the nationalist movement may be seen in the Government of India Act of 1935, which provides for a system of responsible government and for a constitution of which the foundation is the belief that the ultimate source of authority is the people. The provision made for an all-India federation is witness to the extent to which the essential unity of India is being realized, while the institution of a system of government designed to express the common will of the people of British India is a measure of their political education, though this has not gone far in the case of the rural masses. As stated in 1938 by the late Maharaja Gaekwar of Baroda, the administration is in the hands of the educated classes, but the masses have hardly been touched by the new ideas. The change in the position of the governing and governed races is evident both from the transfer of power from British to Indian hands and from the special provisions it has been thought necessary to make for the protection of British interests. Even the most careless observer cannot fail to notice how members of the former ruling race serve in subordinate capacities under Ministers throughout the provinces of British India and how they carry out their duty according to the Church of England catechism, honouring and obeying all that are in authority under the King, and ordering themselves lowly and reverently to their betters. Great, however, as is the advance, it is far from satisfying the demands of nationalists. The right wing maintains that India should have dominion status within the British Empire on the basis of the Westminster Statute. The left wing demands the complete severance of the British connexion and full independence (*purna swaraj*), and many already confidently affirm that the days of the British in India are numbered.

The demand for a western form of government was no doubt due to a genuine conviction of its merits on the part of some, and those the most influential, political leaders, but their views were not shared by others, who doubted whether such a government would be suited to the genius of the people of India, but had no constructive suggestions as to what other form of government could be adopted. Moreover, there was a general feeling that in any case the British people would not agree to any but a democratic system. Responsible government of the modern western type accordingly came into general acceptance because no other model was proposed by any responsible group and because it seemed the

[2] E. S. Montagu and Lord Chelmsford, *Report on Indian Constitutional Reforms* (1918), para. 144.

only avenue of approach to the goal of national government, i.e., the government of British India by Indians. Until recently there was no demand for the institution of a similar system in the States, which are under Indian rulers and have not reached the same stage of political development as British India, though a certain number of the Princes in the larger States had taken steps in the direction of constitutional government by establishing representative assemblies or legislative councils. There is now an incipient demand for a fuller measure of responsible government in the States, a demand which is beginning to be voiced by those living within them as well as by the politicians of British India. Ideas overleap territorial boundaries and the political movement in British India has reactions in the States themselves, the people of which are to some extent beginning to desire that the free institutions established across the border should be reproduced in the Princes' territories. The demand is still somewhat tenuous and unco-ordinated, but it has led to unrest in some States, and some of the ruling Princes have already undertaken to revise the constitutions of their States. The pace of the movement is being forced by agitation due to the Congress party, which is anxious to secure political conformity. It is being proclaimed that the system of government in the States must be assimilated to that of British India, and that there should be no half-way house between autocracy and responsible government. There are those who look forward to the time when the distinction between British India and the India of the Princes will have ceased and there will be only an India of the Indian people; and though some would retain the Princes in the position of constitutional rulers, the more extreme would sweep them away as effete institutions.

The Mechanism of British Rule

KATE L. MITCHELL

Britain has ruled India for more than 150 years, and not the least remarkable thing about that rule is that it has been accomplished with such a relatively small administrative force. According to the 1931 Census, there were 168,000 British in India, of whom 60,000 were in the army, 21,000 in business or professional occupations, and 12,000 in the civilian government services. In other words, less than 100,000 were directly engaged in the task of ruling India, or about 1 for every 4,000 Indians. Even with the total disarmament of the Indian people, and the fact that the most important sections of the army — artillery, tanks, and air force — are kept exclusively in British hands, it is obvious that this small number could not possibly rule 390,000,000 people by power alone. Other instruments were essential, and India stands as perhaps the greatest monument to British skill in devising administrative techniques for preserving control over a vast, alien, and frequently hostile population.

One of these techniques has already been discussed, namely the policy employed with reference to religious and political minorities which, in practice, served to perpetuate communal divisions and to split and weaken nationalist sentiment. Another highly effective technique has been to create a vested interest in the maintenance of British rule

Reprinted from *India without Fable* by Kate L. Mitchell, pp. 47–62, by permission of Alfred A. Knopf, Inc. Copyright © 1942 by Alfred A. Knopf, Inc.

among certain sections of the Indian population, such as the Indian members of the army and civil service, the large landowners who hold their titles from the State, and the Indian Princes, whose power, privileges, and security against internal rebellion are guaranteed by the British Crown. Finally, the British Government has met the rising challenge of Indian nationalism by a series of constitutional reforms providing for the establishment of representative legislative assemblies, but at the same time refusing to allow these bodies to deal with any matters affecting British interests or the basic organization of the British regime, e.g., finance, military expenditures, foreign affairs, police, or tariff policies.

The Government of British India. British India . . . comprises about 55% of the total area of India and contains approximately three-quarters of the population. It is ruled directly by the British Government through the Secretary of State for India in London and the Governor-General (or Viceroy) in New Delhi. Since the federal provisions of the 1935 constitution have never been put into effect, the form of the Central Government of British India is still that established by the India Act of 1919. Power is centralized in the Governor-General and his appointed Executive Council, each member of which serves as a Minister in charge of some branch of the Administration, without responsibility to the Central Legislature.

This Legislature is composed of two Chambers — the Council of State and the Legislative Assembly. The former has a membership of up to sixty, of which thirty-four are chosen by an electorate limited by high property qualifications to about 17,000, while the balance are nominated by the Government. The Legislative Assembly, composed on a communal basis, contains 145 seats distributed as follows:

		Seats
Nominated:	Civil Servants	26
	Others	15
Elected:	Non-Moslems	52
	Moslems	30
	Sikhs	2
	Europeans	9
	Landlords	7
	Commerce and Industry	4
		145

The electorate for the Legislative Assembly too, is restricted by property qualifications; the franchise being held by slightly more than one million, or approximately four-tenths of one per cent of the population of British India.

The Central Legislature deals with questions affecting British India as a whole, and with local government in areas where Provincial Governments do not exist. The Governor-General, however, has unlimited over-riding powers to veto any act of the Legislature and to enforce the passage of legislation which he considers essential. He may also prevent the introduction of legislation affecting finance, religion, defense, and foreign affairs. Approximately 80% of the Central Budget, e.g., army appropriations, debt interest, major salaries, etc., is not subject to vote by the Legislature. With regard to votable expenditure, the Governor-General can, and frequently does, restore a rejected item to the Finance Bill and declare it passed. In addition, the Civil Service and the Indian Police are controlled entirely by the Governor-General in Council.

Within the eleven Provinces of British India, the form of government is that established by the Government of India Act of 1935, which provided for a considerable degree of "Provincial Autonomy." The Governor of each Province, appointed by the British Government, is assisted by a Council of Indian Ministers responsible to an elected legislature. Although the new franchise, based on educational and property qualifications, excludes the poverty-stricken and illiterate majority of the population, thirty-four million were given the right to vote, as against nine million under the previous constitution of 1919. However, these Legislative Assemblies are composed on a communal basis, with nineteen separate categories of voters, and with specially weighted representation for certain minorities. Although the Indian Ministries are nominally authorized to deal with such matters as education, public health, agricultural improvement, local taxation, and the maintenance of law and order, their actual power is strictly limited, since the Provincial Governors hold over-riding powers similar to those of the Governor-General in the Central Government. The Governors also have certain "special responsibilities" in the discharge of which they are responsible only to the Governor-General. These include the maintenance of law and order, the protection of minorities, etc., for which the Governors may take any action they think necessary. Finally, if a Governor should fail to find Ministers willing to conduct the Government "on lines consistent with the discharge of his special responsibility," he can declare the constitution suspended and "assure to himself all such powers as he judges requisite to retrieve the situation."

The Indian Princes. One of the principal results of the famous Mutiny of 1857 was that the British abandoned the policy of annexing native principalities. That Mutiny arose in the annexed territories, and it was the native rulers of the unannexed territories who remained aloof and, in some cases, even aided the British authorities. The lesson was quickly learned, and the Queen's Proclamation of 1858 stated that "we desire no extension of our present territorial possessions. . . . We shall respect the rights, dignity, and honour of the Native Princes as our own." Lord Canning, Governor-General of India in 1860, described the aim of this policy as follows: "It was long ago said by Sir John Malcolm that if we made all India into *Zillahs* (British Districts) it was not in the nature of things that our Empire should last fifty years; but that if we could keep up a number of Native States without political power, but as royal instruments, we should exist in India as long as our naval suprem-

acy was maintained. Of the substantial truth of this opinion I have no doubt; and the recent events have made it more deserving of our attention than ever."

Seventy years later, Professor Rushbrook-Williams, an important Government spokesman on behalf of the Princes, reiterated this view: "The rulers of the Native States are very loyal to the British connection. Many of them owe their very existence to British justice and arms. . . . Their affection and loyalty are important assets for Britain in the present troubles and the readjustments that must come. . . . The situation of these feudatory States, checkerboarding all India as they do, is a great safeguard. It is like establishing a vast network of friendly fortresses in debatable territory. It would be difficult for a general rebellion against the British to sweep India because of this network of powerful loyal Native States."

The States are, of course, unmitigated autocracies, and the assurance of British protection has relieved their rulers of fear of popular rebellion. . . .

For a long period after the Mutiny, British policy was to keep the Princes isolated not only from British India but also from each other. It was only after the rise of the nationalist movement that cooperation among the Princes was encouraged. During the First World War, amidst great anxiety over the growing unrest in India, the establishment of a Chamber of Princes was suggested, and this body was formally inaugurated in 1921. The 109 rulers entitled to salutes of eleven guns or more, are members of the Chamber in their own right; 126 minor states elect twelve representatives; and the petty principalities, about 325 in all, are not represented. The Chamber is a purely consultative body and has no legislative powers. . . .

India in 1930 was shaken by the great civil disobedience campaign, by strikes and boycotts, and other manifestations of a rising popular movement, while the British Government was in the hands, among others, of Mr. Ramsay Macdonald and Mr.

Wedgewood Benn, whom the Princes erroneously suspected of favoring a policy of independence for India. The Princes and their ministers therefore flocked to London in great numbers to attend the Round Table Conference of 1930, and expressed their willingness to enter a Federal Government for India, provided their internal sovereignty would be guaranteed and the obligations of the British Crown to protect them would remain unaltered.

Conservative British opinion seized upon this offer as the ideal solution for the problem of Indian constitutional reform. With the "stabilizing" weight of the Princes in the Central Government, it might be safe to permit a degree of self-government in the Provinces of British India. Thus the Government of India Act of 1935 was drawn up to provide for a Federal Government in which the Princes were given strong representation in the Central Legislature. That the Federal Provisions of the 1935 Act are not yet in force is due to the strong opposition of virtually all sections of opinion in British India, and the fact that the Princes themselves felt that the provisions did not adequately safeguard their power and privileges.

The Indian Civil Service. In the administration of British India, the British Government has built up an extensive and powerful bureaucracy, which is usually described as the most efficient and responsible civil service in the world. . . . Until 1919, the civil service literally governed British India, and even after the introduction of a degree of provincial self-government in the recent constitutional reform measures, the power of the Central Government Services such as the I.C.S. (Indian Civil Service) and the Indian Police remains virtually unrestricted.

Before 1887 practically no Indians were employed in any important positions in the Services. Since that date, the British Government has responded to Indian demands by gradually extending Indian participation, although the admission of Indians to the higher ranks is of fairly recent date, and

all key positions are still retained in British hands. The subordinate central services and provincial services are now predominantly Indian in personnel, e.g., the Civil Medical Department, the Forest Services, the Engineering Department, etc. And even in the political directorate at the top, which is called the Indian Civil Service as distinct from the minor services, there are now only 585 Englishmen as against 617 Indians. The I.C.S. is probably the most privileged civil service in the world. It enjoys enormous prestige, and its members receive high salaries, many special allowances, long leaves of absence, and extremely generous pensions. Control of the I.C.S. rests entirely with the Governor-General, and the protection of its "rights" from popular interference is one of the "special responsibilities" of the Governor-General and the Provincial Governments.

This "Indianization" of the administrative machine, although originally undertaken with reluctance by the British authorities, and still frowned upon by British Civil Servants of the old school who tend to be highly sceptical of Indian efficiency, has nevertheless proved one of the most effective methods by which Britain has enlisted Indian support for British rule. By offering secure careers, high pay, and other privileges, the British have been able to transform a large percentage of the Indian educated class into their agents, including many who might otherwise have been leaders of the nationalist movement. Most British spokesmen claim that this "Indianization" of the civil services was consciously undertaken to prepare the Indian people for self-government, but its effect has actually been to enlist Indian support for a British-controlled administration which, in the opinion of Indian nationalists, is a very different thing.

The attitude of the Indian nationalists toward "Indianization" is perhaps best explained by a quotation from Jawaharlal Nehru's *Autobiography.* Nehru is discussing the need for Indian unity and a common national outlook, and makes the following point: "If we think in terms of the existing political and economic structure and merely wish to tamper with it here and there, to reform it, to 'Indianize' it, then all real inducement to joint action is lacking. The object then becomes one of sharing in the spoils, and the third and controlling party inevitably plays the dominant role, and hands out its gifts to the prize boys of its choice. Only by thinking in terms of a different political framework . . . can we build up a stable foundation for joint action. The whole idea underlying the demand for independence was this: to make people realize that we were struggling for an entirely different political structure and not just an Indianized edition (with British control behind the scenes) of the present order, which Dominion Status signifies."

India's Armed Forces. Although the Indian Civil Service is usually described as the "steel frame" of British administration, the ultimate basis of British rule in India has always been the Indian Army. Few Americans have any clear idea of the organization of this Army, and are consequently both perplexed and irritated by the present attitude of Indian nationalists [during World War II. — ED.] toward the question of their country's defense. A brief sketch of the composition and functions of the Indian Army may serve to indicate at least a few of the reasons why the Indian leaders have been so insistent in their demands for a share in the organization of India's defense, and for the right to train and arm the Indian people for resistance.

In the first place, the process of "Indianization" has not been extended to the higher ranks of the Army. According to Sir Valentine Chirol, the eminent English historian of Indian affairs, "that Army can in fact only be called Indian in the sense that it is recruited from Indians, chiefly of the races reputed for their martial qualities, and that it has a corps of native officers who are seldom more than glorified non-commissioned officers, promoted mostly from the ranks, and who, whatever their seniority

may be, automatically take rank under and receive orders from the youngest British subaltern in the regiment. . . . The Indian Army has such a fine record of gallantry and loyalty that it would be invidious to compare it to a merely mercenary force, but it is essentially a great fighting engine, British-made, British-driven, and British-controlled, for which India provides only the raw material of men."[1]

Sir Valentine then proceeds to refer indirectly to the other major Indian grievance regarding the Army of occupation, when he states that "the whole question of the Indianization of the Army is further aggravated by the fact that military expenditure is itself much the heaviest of all the burdens to be borne by the Indian taxpayer . . . who has no means of controlling the amount or the purposes to which it is applied."

The real nature of the military burden borne by the people of India is seldom appreciated. Such oft-repeated phrases as "Britain's heavy responsibility for India's defense" have served to conceal the simple but astonishing fact that the Indian people have been compelled to tolerate an imperial army for avowedly imperial purposes largely at Indian expense. The British Government has always attached great importance to India as a base of operations, and as a training ground for imperial troops, but so successfully have these aims been translated as "responsibilities" for Indian security that few people outside India are aware that the Indian people have not only paid a major share of the cost of defending British interests in all parts of Asia, but have also paid for the support of a large force of "internal security troops" whose chief function is to crush any attempt on the part of the Indian people to overthrow British rule.

The present organization of the Indian Army dates back to the Mutiny of 1857, and reflects the violent distrust of Indian troops which it engendered in the minds of the British authorities. "The lessons taught

[1] Sir Valentine Chirol, *India*. London: Ernest Benn, Ltd., 1926, pp. 277–79.

by the Mutiny have led to the maintenance of two great principles, of retaining in the country an irresistible force of British troops, and of keeping the artillery in the hands of Europeans."[2] The Indian Army was thus converted definitely into an army of occupation, with Englishmen in the key positions, and these principles have been strictly adhered to, with the tank corps and the air force added to the artillery as exclusively British preserves.

The ratio of British to Indian soldiers has altered from time to time, but has usually been about two British to every five Indians, and the Indian troops are carefully selected and arranged so as to prevent the growth of any solidarity among them. For, as the Punjab Committee on Reorganization advised in their report of 1858, "next to the grand counterpoise of a sufficient European force, comes the counterpoise of natives against natives." Here we have the origin of the myth of the "martial races" from which Indian troops are selected, namely the Gurkhas from Nepal, the Sikhs, the Punjabi Moslems, and certain tribes like the Pathans from the foothills of the Himalayas. These troops are "neatly grouped into battalions, companies, . . . and sometimes even platoons of specified classes (based on tribal, sectarian and caste distinctions) according to a fixed ratio, and no one who does not belong to one of these classes is allowed to enter the army simply because he is physically fit. . . . These groups are so arranged that they retain their tribal or communal loyalties."[3] The Indian Army is therefore in no sense representative of the Indian people as a whole, and many of the troops, like the Gurkhas and Pathans, have little feeling of loyalty to India as a country.

At the outbreak of the present war, the Indian Army was divided into the Field Army, organized for service abroad, in which the proportion of British troops was about one to three (12 British infantry battalions to 36 Indian); the Covering Troops, mainly Indian, used for keeping "order" on the Northwest Frontier; and the Internal Security Troops, which acted as the real army of occupation, and were composed of five British for every four Indians (28 British infantry battalions to 27 Indian). In none of these forces, however, do the Indian troops constitute an independent fighting unit. They are trained and led by British officers, they are dependent on the British artillery, tank, and air force units, and their functions and duties are laid down for them by the British High Command. They are, as Sir Valentine Chirol points out, a purely professional machine under British control.

Obviously, so long as the military organization of India was envisaged in terms of an army of occupation whose primary function was "the suppression of revolutionary movements, both violent and non-violent, organized and designed to upset the established Government," there could be no possibility of developing a genuinely Indian army to take its place. The British authorities have, in fact, placed themselves in the illogical position of saying that India could not be granted self-government because she could not undertake her own defense, and at the same time taking every precaution to make sure that the Indian Army under British control should be the only armed force in the country. The Indian people as a whole are completely disarmed, and no form of military training is open to them. It is still a severe penal offense for an Indian civilian to possess a gun or any other weapon.

[2] Report of Commission on Indian Army Reorganization, 1879. Quoted by G. T. Garratt in *An Indian Commentary*, Jonathan Cape & Harrison Smith, New York, 1929, p. 202.

[3] N. C. Chandhary, *Defence of India*, Allahabad, 1935, p. 32.

THE POLITICAL ASPECT (II)

In this section, three authors present their views on the relationship of British policy to Hindu-Muslim differences in India. The first reading is from "A Report on the Constitutional Problem in India Submitted to the Warden and Fellows of Nuffield College, Oxford," which was prepared in 1942 by Sir Reginald Coupland. It is followed by a selection from *National Movement and Constitutional Development* (1959) by Rama Nand Aggarwala (1913–   ), head of the Political Science Department, Ramjas College, Delhi. The section concludes with a brief excerpt from *Subject India* (1943) by H. N. Brailsford (1873–1958), a veteran British journalist associated with the Independent Labour Party.

Hindu-Moslem Antagonism

SIR REGINALD COUPLAND

THE reason for the persistent refusal of British statesmen to contemplate the development of parliamentary government in India was frequently and plainly stated. It was the familiar fact that India was inhabited by a number of different races and divided by conflicting creeds and ways of life. There were other obstacles to the growth of a democratic system — the backwardness and ignorance of the vast majority of the population and the social barriers of the Hindu caste-system. But these obstacles by themselves would not have seemed insuperable. . . . The major difficulty was the conflict of religions, in particular the clash of Hinduism with Islam. . . .

What are the basic causes of the feud? It is not a conflict of race. In the North-West, it is true, many Indian Moslems are descended from the Arabs, Afghans and Turks who invaded India centuries ago, but elsewhere the vast majority are of native Indian origin, the progeny of those Indians who were converted to their conquerors' faith. . . . The main distinction is not physical, but cultural. It is the outcome of two sharply contrasted religions and of the social systems, the ways of life and thought, they have inspired. Hinduism has its primeval roots in a land of rivers and forests, Islam in the desert. Hindus worship many Gods, Moslems only one: the temple, with its luxuriance of sculptured effigies, confronts the mosque, declaring by its bare simplicity that idolatry is sin. Hinduism maintains a rigid caste-system: Islam proclaims the equal brotherhood of all believers. The classical language of Hindus is Sanskrit, of Moslems Arabic and Persian: the distinctive daily speech of the one is the Hindi, of the other the Urdu variant of Hindustani. The contrast lends itself to a wealth of illustration; but perhaps its most striking feature is the fact that, though Hindus and Moslems live side by side all over India, often in the same small village, and though happily in normal times they are good enough neighbours, yet the natural ties of kinship are completely lacking, since both the Koran and the Hindu laws of caste prohibit intermarriage; nor may an orthodox Hindu share his table with a Moslem. It would be easy, no doubt, to overdraw the contrast in ways of life. India

From Sir Reginald Coupland, *The Indian Problem* (London, 1942), I, 28–36. By permission of J. Simmons, literary executor of Sir Reginald Coupland.

has imposed a certain community of living on all her children, and a stranger to the country, seeing Hindus and Moslems together, in society or professional life, at work or at play, might find it difficult to distinguish them. Yet, under the surface, the gulf remains. The present President of the Central Assembly, Sir Abdur Rahim, once complained that, whereas Indian Moslems felt quite at home in the Moslem countries of Asia, "in India we find ourselves in all social matters total aliens when we cross the street and enter that part of the town where our Hindu fellow-townsmen live."

History has intensified the sense of difference; for the Moslems remember that they were once the conquering and ruling people and the Hindus their subjects, paying the *jizya* or tax exacted from all non-Moslems. There had been great chapters in the annals of India long before the rise of Islam; but in Moslem eyes the glories of the Maurya or the Gupta Empire had been eclipsed by that of the Moguls. Never had India been so powerful and prosperous, so well-governed, or so famous throughout the world as in the days of Akbar. . . .

The splendour of that age seemed all the brighter by contrast with the long period of decline and decay that followed it. The decline was both economic and political. Once the Moslems had been lords of the land in every sense, but with the coming of the rule of law they began to lose their grasp of it. The big estates were thinned away by extravagance and litigation, and the small man was increasingly enmeshed and dispossessed of his holding by the moneylender who, since usury is banned by the Koran, was more often than not a Hindu. In all the new economic developments of the later nineteenth century, moreover, the more conservative and less educated Moslems were no match for the keen, purposeful, better organised Hindus. Still more marked was the change in the political status of the Moslems. With the collapse of the Mogul Empire and the advent of British rule they ceased to be the governing

class. The ranks of the Indian army, it is true, were increasingly filled with Moslems. The north-west corner of India was the chief centre of the Moslem population, and the Moslems, therefore, with the Sikhs, regarded themselves as the warders of India's one dangerous frontier. But all military command was now in British hands. It was the same with all the important posts in the civil administration of British India. Even in the lower ranks of public service, moreover, the Moslems soon found themselves edged out by the Hindus. Their first setback was the dropping of Persian as the official language; the next was the Mutiny, which was wrongly supposed at the time to have been mainly due to Moslem instigation; the third was the growth of higher education, the opportunities and professional rewards of which were eagerly seized by the Hindus but rejected by the Moslems, who clung to the old orthodox tradition of religious education and turned their backs on the impious new learning of the "Franks." Thus the Moslems failed to share in the intellectual renaissance which the acquisition of the English language, and of the knowledge of Western science and thought which it conveyed, was bringing about in Hindu India.

It was the connexion between education and government that forced the Moslems to bestir themselves. When Hindu clerks were promoted to posts in which they could give orders, when even policemen were chosen because they were good at their books, it was clearly wise for Moslems to reconsider their attitude to the new education. That was the doctrine preached by the greatest Indian Moslem of the time, Sir Syed Ahmad Khan. Defying orthodox hostility, he declared that modern learning was neither forbidden by the Koran nor dangerous to the faith it taught; and by the courage of his convictions and the strength of his personality he gradually obtained an unrivalled hold on Moslem opinion throughout India. The climax of his work was reached at the foundation in 1877 of a Moslem college, now a university, at

Aligarh. That marked the turning of the tide, the end of the decline and the beginning of a recovery. But the Moslems have still to make up for lost time. The level of education in their community is not yet as high as the Hindu level; and it is significant that, since the introduction of competitive examinations held in India for entrance to the higher civil services, a number of places have always been reserved for nomination in order to maintain a sufficient proportion of Moslems and other minority communities in the official corps.

It was this relative backwardness in education, coupled with the knowledge that they were only about one-quarter of the Indian population as a whole, that accounted for the indifference, if not antagonism, with which most Moslems watched the growth of the Indian nationalist movement. Nationalism feeds on memories, but the memories of Moslems were more concerned with Islam than with India: they did not share their Hindu fellow-countrymen's pride in a record of civilisation stretching far into the past; and not among Moslems only the birth of a new political self-consciousness tended to revive and strengthen the old communal loyalties as much as to inspire a new devotion to India as the motherland of them all. Political agitation, moreover, was concentrated, as has been seen, on the demand for representative government of the British kind, and that, as Sir Syed Ahmad warned his fellow-Moslems, meant "majority rule," with the Hindus in the greater part of India always in power and the Moslems never. It is not surprising, therefore, that the Congress, despite its national title and appeal, proved to be a predominantly Hindu body. . . . The growing influence of the Congress and the attention paid to it by Government were a lesson Moslems could not miss. Once more, it seemed, they were in danger of being left behind. The knowledge that a new instalment of "Reforms" was under consideration spurred them to action, and, since most of their leaders were unwilling to make common

cause with the Congress, a separate political organisation for Indian Moslems was created — the All-India Moslem League. Its first conference was held in December, 1906.

The Moslem leaders were faced by the fact that, since the Act of 1892, not only the principle of representation but also in practice the principle of election had been established in the constitution of the Provincial legislatures; and they realised that the forthcoming advance was likely to confirm and extend the elective principle. To meet that situation they had two clear points of policy. First, in all elections, whether for the Legislative Councils or for local bodies, the Moslems must be separately represented and their representatives separately elected by purely Moslem electors. Second, the extent of the Moslem community's representation must be "commensurate not merely with their numerical strength, but also with their political importance and the value of the contribution which they make to the defence of the Empire." These were the main points of the Moslem case which was submitted to Lord Minto [in 1906], shortly before the first meeting of the League, by a Moslem deputation, headed by its president, the Aga Khan. The Viceroy's response was wholly sympathetic. He did not commit himself to any particular method of election, but "I am as firmly convinced," he said, "as I believe you to be that any electoral representation in India would be doomed to mischievous failure which aimed at granting a personal enfranchisement regardless of the beliefs and traditions of the communities composing the population of this continent." The Secretary of State concurred; he tentatively suggested a scheme for a joint electoral college, but he did not press it; and in due course the Moslems found their two demands conceded in the Act of 1909 and the regulations made under it. The Moslems were given what was later to be known as "weightage," *i.e.*, more seats than they were entitled to by numbers only, and, while voting also in "general" constituencies side by side with Hindus, they were to vote for their own members in separate and wholly Moslem constituencies. That their anxieties were not wholly allayed, however, was shown by their objection to the appointment to the Viceroy's Executive Council of a single Indian, who was naturally a Hindu. But on this point their protests were overruled. The issue did not arise on the appointment of Indians to the Secretary of State's Council, since there were two of them and one was a Moslem.

The creation of communal electorates was a flagrant breach of democratic principle, as Morley was well aware; but there was force in the argument stressed by the Moslem leaders that, in the present state of Indian feeling, to make Moslem seats dependent on Hindu votes, so far from tending to make both communities conscious of a common citizenship, would embitter the existing antagonism and convert every election into a dangerous battleground. Nor, as they pointed out, would the mere "reservation" of seats for Moslems secure their faithful representation unless only Moslems voted for them, since the Hindu votes would go to the candidate who identified himself least wholeheartedly with the interests of his own community. It was a strong case, and the weight of Moslem opinion behind it could not be ignored. Nor, after all, was Morley doing violence to his democratic conscience. His ideas of Indian government, as has been seen, had nothing to do with democracy.

The attitude of the Hindu nationalists — and there were some, though not at this time many, Moslems who supported the Congress — was naturally quite different. At the session of 1910 the Congress, "while recognising the necessity of providing a fair and adequate representation in the Legislative Councils for the Muhammadan and other communities where they are in a minority," condemned the method of separate electorates and demanded the removal of "anomalous restrictions between different sections of His Majesty's subjects in the matter of the franchise." It would be illogi-

cal to criticise this attitude. The Hindus, after all, were the great majority — at least two-thirds — of the Indian people, and their traditions went back to the dawn of Indian history. If India were to be governed by counting votes, they could scarcely be expected to surrender the rights their numbers gave them. More questionable was the growing tendency to minimise the gravity of Hindu-Moslem schism, and to assert that it was largely due to British rule and would cease to be a serious matter if India were allowed to govern herself. It was often pointed out that Hindu-Moslem disorders rarely, if ever, occurred in the Indian States; and the British Government was even charged with deliberately trying to maintain and deepen the feud on the principle of *divide et impera*. "This quarrel is not old," said Mr. Gandhi at the Round Table Conference in 1931: ". . . I dare to say it is co-eval with the British advent." He could scarcely have intended those words to bear their full meaning, but there was half a truth in them. For the open exhibition of the quarrel, the throwing-off of all restraint, the rioting and fighting — none of this was possible under Mogul rule. Akbar set Hindus on a formal equality with Moslems, but the Hindus would no more have dared in his day than in Aurungzeb's to assert their communal rights or in any way to challenge or provoke the feelings of their rulers. For several reasons the position has been very different under British rule. The Government, to begin with, has been neither Hindu nor Moslem: the expression of communal loyalty, therefore, has not been in itself a defiance of authority, but only when it has led to a breach of the peace. The British rule of law, moreover, coupled with a policy of freedom for all creeds, has given the communities a sense of security and self-confidence which no Indian autocracy could give them. Finally, it is the gradual introduction of the British form of self-government — and this is what differentiates British India most markedly from the Indian States — that has steadily intensified the conflict; for, once majority rule was in sight, it became a struggle for power. And, since this conflict has been the cause of British hesitation in the past to advance India along the road to freedom, and since it is the cause of the present halt when the goal is almost within reach, it is also the cause of the continuance of British rule. But Britain did not light the fire, nor has she been doing the devil's work of stoking it. Mr. Muhammad Ali, who with his brother led the Caliphate Movement in 1921, was no friend or apologist of British rule in India, but the judgment he passed on the Hindu-Moslem schism at the Round Table Conference was less misleading than Mr. Gandhi's. "It is the old maxim of 'divide and rule,'" he said. "But there is a division of labour here. *We* divide and *you* rule."[1]

[1] *Indian Round Table Conference*, First Session (1930–1), 102. In her *India, Minto and Morley* (London, 1934, p. 47) Lady Minto quotes a letter she received from an official describing the Viceroy's response to the Moslem deputation (p. 34, above) as "nothing less than the pulling back of sixty-two millions of people from joining the ranks of the seditious opposition." It may well be true that many Moslems, if their claim for separate electorates had been rejected, might have joined the Hindu extremists in attacking the Government; but there is no evidence to suggest that the deputation was in any sense engineered. It was actually organised by the well-known Moslem leader, Nawab Mahsin-ul-Mulk, shortly before he died. Nor was the Moslem opposition to an unqualified representative system on the British model a novelty in 1908. As early as 1883, Syed Ahmad, speaking on Lord Ripon's introduction of elections to local bodies, declared that "election pure and simple" was quite unsuited to diversified India where "the rigour of religious institutions has kept even neighbours apart." ...

"Divide-and-Rule" Tactics

RAMA NAND AGGARWALA

MOHAMMEDANS had ruled over India centuries before she passed into the hands of the British. As ex-rulers of India before the British, Muslims had acquired a certain degree of superiority complex in their attitude towards the Hindus. Later, as a conquered race, they nursed a good deal of resentment against the British rule. Hence it was difficult for them to reconcile themselves to their subordinate position under the British masters.

In between the two communities, *i.e.*, the Hindus and Muslims, the policy followed by the East India Company, to start with, was that of favouring the Hindus. This was natural because the British looked upon Muslims as permanently hostile to their rule. As the result of this policy, the Company began to oust Muslims from all positions of importance and from every walk of life, including the government jobs. The destruction of indigenous or cottage industries in India at the hands of the Company adversely affected mostly Muslims. The educational policy of the Company also proved detrimental to their interests, because the Muslims failed to take advantage of it. "In the army their recruitment was limited, in arts and crafts they were crippled and rendered helpless."

The Wahabi Movement: The Wahabi movement which started in Arabia towards the end of the 18th century had an encouraging effect on the Indian Muslims. The

From Rama Nand Aggarwala, *National Movement and Constitutional Development* (2nd ed.; Delhi, 1956), pp. 59–63. By permission of the author and of Metropolitan Book Co., Private Limited, Delhi.

movement was purely religious in the beginning and was brought to India by Saiyyid Ahmed Brelvi. When it began to spread in India, it gave new hope and ambition to the depressed Muslims, who felt elevated at the glorification of their religion. In India, the movement soon acquired a popular and revolutionary character, because it preached hatred against a foreign master and came handy to Muslims, who were groaning under the British rule. In short, Wahabism fanned the flame of communalism and anti-British feeling in Muslims. The British rulers of India became naturally the enemies of the Movement and it was ruthlessly crushed as seditious. But before it finally died, it had served as one of the causes responsible for the outbreak of the Mutiny. . . . It was commonly believed by the British Government that the Mutiny was mostly engineered by Muslims and, therefore, the Government became even more anti-Muslim after the Mutiny. . . .

Work of Sir Syed: Sir Syed Ahmed was the man who was mostly responsible for bridging the gulf between Muslims and the British rulers and also for infusing in them a desire to acquire the Western education. He entered service under the Company in 1837 and during the Mutiny proved a loyal friend of the British. In 1869, he visited England and was much impressed by the liberal English education. In 1876, he retired from Government service and decided to devote the rest of his life to the service of his community. In pursuance of this aim, he founded a Mohammedan Anglo-Oriental College at Aligarh, which became the nursery of the educated modern-minded Muslims and became the focal centre of the Aligarh movement of later years.

Sir Syed Ahmed advised Muslims to keep aloof from the Congress, because in his opinion the Anglo-Muslim alliance was more profitable for the Muslim community than cooperation with the Hindus in the national agitation. In 1887, he organised the Muslim Educational Conference, which began to hold its sessions, like the Congress, every year. In 1888, when the Congress became a suspect in the eyes of the Government, he founded the Patriotic Association in league with Raja Shiva Prasad of Benaras, with the set purpose of opposing the Congress and to counteract its activities. In his early days, Sir Syed gave ample proof of his nationalist views. By the eighties of the 19th century, Sir Syed had become an arch enemy of the Congress and a rank communalist. It is usually believed that the change was brought about mainly by Mr. Beck, the English principal of the Aligarh College, who misled Sir Syed into "believing that while an Anglo-Muslim alliance would ameliorate the condition of the Muslim community, joining the nationalist agitation would lead them once again to sweat, toil and tears." Whatever the reason, immediately after the birth of the Indian National Congress, Sir Syed began to work in a manner which certainly weakened the national forces.

Policy of divide and rule: We have already noted in one of the preceding chapters that the attitude of friendly neutrality which the Government had assumed towards the Congress at the time of its birth very soon gave place to one of active hostility. In 1888, during the fourth session of the Congress at Allahabad, the change in the attitude of the Government was quite apparent. For the Government, its future line of action was obvious. If they were to counteract the growing power of the Congress, they must find friend[s] among the Muslims and start the policy of divide and rule. This sinister policy was started through Mr. Beck, the principal of the Aligarh College, whom Sir John Strachey described as, "An Englishman, who was engaged in Empire-building activities in a far-off land." In 1889, Mr. Beck sponsored a memorial of Muslims against the Bill introduced by Charles Bradlaugh with the object of introducing representative institutions in India. In 1893, the Mohammedan Anglo-Oriental Defence Association was formed with the active help of the Government to counteract the growing popularity of the Congress.

The policy of divide and rule was now started by the Government. The Congress was to be weakened by encouraging Muslims. The traditional anti-Muslim policy of the Government was now reversed and it became anti-Hindu. When, towards the beginning of the 20th century, the Extremists began to make their weight felt, the Government was exasperated still more and they adopted the Machiavellian game, even more blatantly. In 1905 the Partition of Bengal was proposed and executed. Whatever the official excuse for the Partition, it was a clever move to drive a wedge between the two communities and to weaken the forces of the Bengal nationalism by weaning away Muslims from the Congress. The policy of divide and rule was intensified after the entry of the Extremists. This was natural in view of the danger, the British Government felt, at the hands of Extremists like Tilak, who led the Congress to pass in 1906 the resolution asking for self-government like that of the United Kingdom or Colonies. The Extremists had openly challenged the Government.

Muslim Deputation of 1906 and Separate Electorates: In the year 1906 something happened, which has coloured the whole subsequent national movement in India and has had far-reaching effects on the Hindu-Muslim relations. In 1906, Lord Minto had formed a Committee to consider the necessity of further reforms for India. This immediately led to a Deputation of Muslims, headed by His Highness the Agha Khan, which met Lord Minto at Simla on October 1, 1906 and claimed separate electorates, i.e., communal representation from the Imperial Legislative Council down to the District Boards and weightage to Muslims as something which was absolutely essential to protect their legitimate interests. Lord Minto was over-ready to accept the demands of the Muslims and said, "The pith of your address as I understand it, is a claim that in any system of representation, whether it affects a Munici-

pality, a District Board or a Legislature, . . . the Mohammedan community would be represented as a body . . . you *justly* claim that your position should be estimated not merely on your numerical strength but in respect to the political importance of your community and service that it has rendered to the Empire. I am entirely in accord. . . . *I am as firmly convinced,* as I believe you to be, that any electoral representation in India *would be doomed to mischievous failure,* which aimed at granting a personal enfranchisement regardless of the beliefs and traditions of the communities composing the population of this continent." The words italicized tell a tale of their own. They show an eagerness to agree, which almost amounts to an encouragement. Thus, the principle of separate electorates was accepted. It was introduced in the 1909 Reforms. The Hindus and Muslims were to vote separately for their respective nominees, as a result of which the Hindus and Muslims were never united in a real manner hereafter, except probably during the days of Khilafat[1] for a short time. Such was the nature of the poison injected by Lord Minto into the body-politic of India. It is, therefore, believed by some that "the real father of Pakistan was not Jinnah or Rahimattoola but Lord Minto."

Part played by Minto: There is a controversy as to whether this Deputation was sponsored by the British bureaucracy and their Anglo-Indian friends or depended on the initiative of Muslims themselves. Maulana Mohammad Ali, in his presidential address to the Congress in 1923 described it as "a command performance." Prof. Coupland, the official historian of the Cripps Mission of 1942, on the other hand states, "There is no evidence to suggest that the Deputation of 1906 was in any sense engineered by the Government.["]

---

[1] *I.e.,* the period of protest among Indian Muslims at the treatment of the Ottoman Empire and the caliphate in the Treaty of Sèvres after World War I; the Muslim "Khilafat movement" worked in close cooperation with Gandhi and the Indian National Congress. [Editor's note]

The following relevant extracts lend support to the conclusion arrived at by Maulana Mohammad Ali: —

(*i*) On May 28, 1906, Lord Minto wrote to Lord Morley, "I have been thinking a good deal lately of a possible counter-poise to Congress aims."

(*ii*) On August 10, 1906, Mr. Archibold, Principal of Aligarh College, wrote to Nawab Mohsun-ul-Mulk, the Secretary of the Aligarh College, "Colonel Dunlop Smith, Private Secretary of His Excellency, is agreeable to receive the Muslim Deputation. He advises that a formal letter requesting permission to wait on His Excellency be sent to him. The formal letter should be sent with the signatures of some representative Muslims. The Deputation should consist of the representatives of all the Provinces. I would here suggest that we begin with a solemn expression of loyalty. The Government decision to take a step in the direction of self-government should be appreciated. But our apprehension should be expressed that the principle of election, if introduced, would prove detrimental to the interest of the Muslim minority. It should respectfully be suggested that nomination or representation by religion be introduced to meet public

opinion . . . but in all these views I must be in the background. They must come from. . . .[2] We must expedite matters."

(*iii*) On the evening of the date of the Deputation, Lady Minto receives the following letter from an official, "I must send your Excellency a line to say that a very big thing has happened today. A work of statesmanship that will affect India and Indian history for many a long year. It is nothing less than the pulling back of 62 millions of people from joining the ranks of the seditious opposition."

(*iv*) On December 6, 1909, Morley wrote to Minto, "I won't follow you again into our Mohammedan dispute. Only I respectfully remind you, once more, that it was your early speech about their extra claims that first started the M. (Mohammedan) hare. I am convinced my decision was best."

(*v*) The biographer of Lord Minto comments on the speech of the Viceroy before the Deputation as follows, "The speech undoubtedly prevented the ranks of sedition being swollen by Muslim recruits and an inestimable advantage in the day of trouble which was dawning.". . .

[2] Omission by the author, probably of a proper name. [Editor's note]

The British Arbiter

H. N. BRAILSFORD

I T would be an evasion to conclude this chapter on Muslims and Hindus without some reference to our own conduct as arbiters. Have we sought to divide and rule? Indians with hardly an exception would answer with an emphatic affirmative: they assume it as a settled fact in all their discussions of our policy and history. Many, perhaps most Americans hold the

same belief. Up to the Mutiny, leading officials under the Company occasionally recommended it as a maxim of policy. English men of business in India will on occasion blurt it out today as an obvious truth which everyone takes for granted. This is not evidence. The situation lends itself inevitably to this suspicion and this interpretation. British rule could not have endured

Reprinted from *Subject India* by H. N. Brailsford (Copyright © 1943, by Henry Noel Brailsford), pp. 114–117, by permission of The John Day Company, Inc., publisher, of Victor Gollancz, Ltd., London, and of Mrs. H. N. Brailsford.

till today, if ever under good leadership the great mass of the two communities had for any length of time combined to end it, as under poor leadership during the Mutiny a part of them did. Can this risk fail to influence the calculations and policies of British statesmen and officials? But where on a crude view of the facts we do seem to be keeping the two apart, an innocent explanation is always possible. Even the most fatal instance, Lord Morley's separate communal electorates, can be excused by reference to a worthy motive. I have heard him defend it in private conversation, though his manner made on me the impression that he was not happy about what he had just done. Would not the two be less likely to quarrel, he argued, if they voted apart: would not contested elections, fought it may be on a low level of courtesy, aggravate their dissensions? If we classify them carefully and tabulate their rights with precision, it is because we mean to hold the scales even between them. Our tradition is that we arbitrate with as near an approach to impartiality as is humanly possible. This is, I do not doubt, a true account of what normally passes in the conscious mind of statesmen and officials. To discover any calculation or any aim more sinister than this, a psychologist would have to peer into the darkness of their sub-conscious processes. That is what Indians habitually do, and like all subject races they have sensitive antennae.

To speculate about motives is an unprofitable exercise. The sober student of this question will prefer to consider results. Two are obvious. In the first place, by classifying Indians according to creed in every conceivable relationship of public life we helped to make them abnormally conscious of their differences. They were haunted by religion — if this be religion — obsessed by it, until every other consideration that can unite men or divide them faded into the background. We labelled them Hindus and Muslims till they forgot they were men. In the second place, by dwelling on these differences and exalting our own function as arbiters, we persuaded ourselves and for a time we even persuaded some Indians that our rule was indispensable. Even now, when events have driven us to promise its early end, this theme of our sacred duty to the minorities constantly recurs in our official statements.

The historian, baffled in the attempt to read our motives, may turn to something less elusive, our political arithmetic. He may be startled, as perhaps the reader of the previous chapter was, when he discovers that Sir Samuel Hoare proposed[1] to give the princes — but not their subjects — a voting power of 40 and 33 per cent in the two chambers of his federal legislature, though these subjects amount to only 23 per cent of the population of the Peninsula. He will marvel at the discovery that Sir Samuel over-estimated Muslims for voting purposes in comparison with Hindus in the proportion of two to one. On further research, he will discover that as usual in India this practice had tradition behind it. Lord Morley in the Morley-Minto reforms did the same thing in a still more staggering disproportion. To acquire a vote a Hindu must pay income tax on an income of Rs. 300,000, while a Muslim could achieve it with an income of Rs. 3,000; a Hindu graduate must have held his degree for thirty years, a Muslim for only three. To this principle the bureaucracy gives the name of weightage. Chivalry and equity require that something should be done to weight the scales in favour of the minority. The historian, pondering on weightage, may next discover in the British Museum some persuasive arguments by Lord Morley in favour of the meticulously accurate system of proportional representation advocated by his friend Lord Courtney. Accuracy is for England, chivalry for India. Pursuing his enquiries, he may find that Mr. Ramsay MacDonald gave his name to some of these Indian communal awards. Now Mr. MacDonald was a somewhat violent

[1] In the federation scheme of the Government of India Act of 1935, which never went into effect. [Editor's note]

opponent of proportional representation. But as I can testify at first hand, his view, which he would express with some heat, was that majorities rather than minorities should be accorded extra representation, in the interests of "strong government." But again, he too was thinking of Great Britain. In his bewilderment, the historian may then go on to scrutinise the minorities thus favoured by Lord Morley, Sir Samuel Hoare and Mr. MacDonald.[2] He will discover them without much trouble, in any of Mr. Churchill's speeches, arrayed on our side against Congress and "the extremists." He may sum up by applauding our "chivalry" — but I am hardly authorised to anticipate his conclusions.

The same historian, when he frames his questions, will have to consider not merely what we said but what we omitted to say. For half-a-century or more, every Secretary of State and every Viceroy has kept in his dispatch-case the notes of a stereotyped statement, which he has repeated with variations on every public occasion. The Simon Report made the case with ponderous detail and at inordinate length. Mr. Churchill will do it with a touch of passion and more than a trace of malice. We all know the pattern of this statement about India. It may mention the many languages and races. It mobilises all the interests opposed

to Congress. It parades the statistics, not always impeccably accurate, of the minorities. And invariably it dwells on the opposed religions and the depressed classes. Sometimes it is done in a tone of fatalistic regret, sometimes with an air of polemical triumph, but always the stress is on the divisions of India. And this India's rulers have been doing for fifty years and for much more than fifty years.

Was this the way to unite the jarring creeds? I can imagine an official speech on wholly different lines. Sometimes with Churchillian eloquence, sometimes with a touch of humour, but always with courtesy and persuasion it would have sought to induce Indians to forget their religious divisions. It might have reminded them that we once had our suspect Catholic minority and our dissenting untouchables. It might have communicated to Muslims and Hindus the discovery our fathers made long ago that creed is an irrelevance in modern politics. It might have asked them whether the Koran and the Vedic Hymns really differ irreconcilably over income tax, the rupee exchange and the best way of combating malaria and hookworm. If every day and in every way, each according to his temperament and opportunities, using the press and the wireless, schoolbooks and white papers, the officials and spokesmen of this mighty government had sought to minimise religious differences and promote an outlook of secular commonsense, and done this steadily for fifty years, is it certain that this feud would rage as it does today? They chose to make the other speech.

---

[2] Chivalry is a subjective principle, and we must be prepared for some caprice. In Mr. MacDonald's award the Hindus profit by it, as well as the Muslims, notably in Sind, where they are a small minority. But in Bengal, where they are a big minority, they are seriously underrepresented. But as everyone knows, Bengali Hindus incline to disloyalty.

TOWARD FREEDOM

In this concluding section, the first two readings focus on the process by which Indian independence was achieved, and the reasons why it was accompanied by partition into the two states of India and Pakistan. The final excerpt offers an analysis of the revolutionary impact of Western domination on Asia in general and India in particular.

E. W. R. Lumby (1909–), the author of *The Transfer of Power in India, 1945–7* (1954), worked in the India Office from 1934 to 1947 and served on the staff of the British Cabinet Mission to India in 1946. Since that time he has taught at the Royal Naval College in Greenwich, where he is now Principal Lecturer in History.

W. Norman Brown (1892–), Professor of Sanskrit and Chairman of the Department of South Asia Regional Studies at the University of Pennsylvania, is perhaps the leading American authority on Indian society and culture. The second excerpt in this section is from his book, *The United States and India and Pakistan* (1953).

K. M. Panikkar (1895–) was educated at Madras Christian College in India and at Oxford University. In a varied career, he has taught history, edited *The Hindustan Times,* and held various governmental offices in princely states prior to Indian independence. Since independence, he has served as India's ambassador to China (1948–1952), to Egypt (1952–53), and to France (since 1956). He has published more than a dozen books on various aspects of Indian history, as well as the more general study, *Asia and Western Dominance: A Survey of the Vasco Da Gama Epoch of Asian History, 1498–1945* (1959), from which the concluding selection is taken.

The Transfer of Power

E. W. R. LUMBY

I n the reaction of the Asiatic peoples to Western expansion during the last century and a half, three phases can, very broadly, be distinguished. In the first, the traditional order hits back blindly at the foreign influences which threaten it, and which are feared all the more because only vaguely understood: the forces of custom and fanaticism are mobilised in a Boxer Rebellion, an Indian Mutiny or an anti-foreign movement such as followed Com-modore Perry's minatory opening-up of Japan in 1853. The second phase begins when the foreign influences have infected the educated minority with western ideas of nationalism and liberal democracy; then the new intelligentsia comes into conflict with its overlords on the question of how far and how fast this exotic political philosophy should be applied to its own country. But as yet, though it may claim to speak for the nation as a whole, it concentrates on

From E. W. R. Lumby, *The Transfer of Power in India, 1945–7* (London, 1954), pp. 9–15, 35–39, 257–261. By permission of George Allen & Unwin, Ltd.

political objectives which may be expected to bring benefit mainly to its own class; the masses remain unaffected. Then, as industrialism and the doctrines of social democracy spread from the West, there grows the belief that if political democracy is to be genuine, it must be accompanied by radical economic changes. In Socialism, the second and third phases are blended. In Communism, which follows it, the emphasis has completely shifted from the political to the economic aspect of life: a section of the educated minority works tirelessly to bring the peasants and factory workers into action against the landlords and capitalists. For now the antagonist is no longer only the foreign invader, but an economic class including natives as well as foreigners. But none the less the Communist phase, like its predecessors, is essentially a reaction against the West; for Communism, though originally a product of western industrial society, preaches that the West is the home of capitalism, a system unsound, corrupt and doomed to destruction. Hence all the ideas and institutions of the West being, according to Communist theory, the product of its vicious economy, must be uncompromisingly rejected.

In India all the three phases have appeared at various times. Hindu and Muslim traditionalism resisted vigorously whenever British rule, departing from its normal policy of neutrality in religious matters, did anything to disturb them. The educated middle class, the motive force of the second phase, has provided the leadership, and a great part of the membership, of the political parties. More recently Socialism and Communism appeared, trying in vain to prevent the national movement from splitting irrevocably on communal lines. Yet Gandhi, the greatest figure in the movement, cannot be fitted into any academic classification. At once traditionalist and innovator, the self-confessed opponent of modern civilisation who nevertheless became the leader of a nationalist movement essentially typical of its age, the propagandist who appeared in the villages as a blend of saint, politician, and sanitary reformer, he combines in his personality some of the characteristics of each phase.

But although in the Indian reaction all the three phases have been intermingled, the second has beyond doubt played the most important part in the rise of the two nationalisms which have developed into the States of India and Pakistan. In the story of the transfer of power, which is told in the following chapters, the educated middle class monopolise the principal roles, whether as individuals or parties; the vast mass of the people is merely passive, except in times of unusual excitement. Admittedly, the educated middle class amounts to no more than a small minority of the population. But those who sneer at them on this account seriously underestimate both the value to their British rulers of the support, or acquiescence, of these people and, more generally, the capital importance of education as a social force. It was the advance of education that enabled similar classes to have such a vast influence on the modern history of Europe and America. Like their French prototype at the time of the Revolution, the middle classes in India were content neither to be ignored nor, as time went on, to cooperate in a subordinate capacity with the British or with a rival community. They demanded nothing less than the sovereign position in the State.

The British response to these varied phenomena was, up to 1917, perplexed, hesitant and at times confused. During the first half of the nineteenth century British statesmen and officials were quite ready to acknowledge that in the long run Indian self-government and even independence were inevitable. In 1818, for instance, Lord Hastings, the Governor-General, even while conducting a policy designed considerably to extend British rule, looked forward to "a time not very remote . . . when England will, on sound principles of policy, wish to relinquish the domination which she has gradually and unintentionally assumed over this country and from which she cannot at present recede." But after the Mutiny, in the atmosphere of imperial pride and of competition for markets and fields for investment, this vision of the future became much less clear. When at length the British began to seek ways of associating Indians with the tasks of government, their policy in this respect was at variance with the educational policy which they had followed since Macaulay's famous Minute of 1835. On the one hand the schools and universities which they founded ignored Indian history and culture in favour of education on the English system and through English as the medium of instruction: and so young Indians were taught to admire the ideas and institutions of Western parliamentary democracy. On the other hand such deliberative or advisory bodies as they established, though these involved the introduction to India of the hitherto unknown devices of representation and election, seemed evidence of a desire not so much to import Western institutions as to build on the indigenous foundation of the *durbar,* or audience, whereat Indian rulers through the centuries had been accustomed to consult their notables and listen to grievances. Even the Morley-Minto reforms of 1909 were in effect an attempt to meet the Indian politicians' demand for Parliamentary institutions by a system of enlarged *durbars* with somewhat wider powers than before. It was only in 1917 that the British Government, yielding to nationalist feeling in India and liberal pressure at home, declared their policy to be "the gradual development of self-governing institutions with a view to the progressive realisation of responsible government in India as an integral part of the British Empire." Here was the beginning of a policy which Britain can claim credit for having followed consistently and faithfully right up to the eventual transfer of power. Two years later the Government of India Act of 1919 remodelled the Central Legislature, giving a wider application to the principles of election and representation: while in the Provinces it partially introduced the principle of ministerial responsibility by entrusting certain departments of government to Indian ministers responsible to the Provincial Legislatures.

But if the British Government was slow to face the implications of the spread to India of Western political ideas, some of the leaders of the Muslim community were more prescient. Already in 1909, if not earlier, they had foreseen that the development of representative institutions would eventually lead to the introduction of a fully-fledged parliamentary system on the British model. Their alarm at this prospect was due to their recognition that it would mean government by ministers responsible to the elected representatives of the majority; and in Indian conditions, they argued, majority rule would be in effect the rule of the Hindu majority, with the Muslim minority in perpetual subordination. In 1909 therefore they asked for and obtained safeguards in the form of separate electorates from which Muslims, and they alone, would elect representatives to seats reserved for their community. This, of course, was radically inconsistent with any comprehensive notion of democracy, embracing as it should not only the principle of majority rule but also the complementary principle that minorities must feel assured of fair treatment at the hands of the majority.

This concession to the Muslims of separate electorates marks the beginning of the Hindu-Muslim conflict in its twentieth-century form of a struggle for political power. Some foreigners, and even some Indians, have taken it at its face value as a religious conflict, such as the world has hardly seen for over two centuries. . . .

But if religion, history and economic competition were the only ingredients in the Hindu-Muslim conflict of the twentieth century, it would be hard to explain why during the previous century, in spite of sporadic communal riots and a certain amount of bickering, the two communities had on the whole lived fairly peacefully side by side. The reason is of course that the political element had not yet been injected into the conflict. The Government, neither Hindu nor Muslim, would arbitrate in the religious quarrels of the two communities; but its neutrality was the result of its being both alien and autocratic, and there was no question of its ceasing to be either in the foreseeable future. Hence the communities had nothing political to quarrel about. India was in fact a country without politics, or at least without party politics.

But this state of affairs could endure only so long as Indian nationalism had not become strong enough to win from the British at least the promise of self-government. As soon as there was any prospect of even a limited transfer of power, there arose the question of who would inherit the power the British would be relinquishing.

There was one obvious claimant. The Indian National Congress had been founded in 1885 as a focus for political discussion; though its members were Indian, it had owed its inspiration largely to a group of Englishmen and had at first enjoyed a certain amount of official approval. But before long it became the most influential opponent of the Government; the foremost representative of Indian nationalism, it was aspiring to be its sole representative. Its aim was in fact to present the British with its demands, first for extended self-government and since 1921 for complete independence, as the demands of the whole Indian people; it would be a vast umbrella, sheltering people of all castes and creeds, of all shades of opinion on domestic political and economic issues. And in this aim it achieved a high degree of success, notably in avoiding being diverted from its nationalist objectives by internal dissensions on economic policy. It recruited big business men, who subsidised it and helped to provide it with a press: smaller business men and professional men, great and small: out-and-out Gandhians who rejected industrialisation and sought to return to the primitive self-supporting village community; Communists, until they finally broke with it in 1945; and Socialists — though

since the coming of independence they too have separated. The strength and cohesion of the party must have surprised even its members, who used to foretell that, since the demand for independence was all that kept it together, so soon as the British withdrew it would split into right and left wings, after the European fashion, on questions of economic organisation. However, events have shown that these prophets were too modest. So far as the Indian Republic is concerned, Congress has proved to be the real inheritor of the British power, and still dominates the government and political life of the country. The elections of 1952 have shown that the operation of universal suffrage under the new Constitution has not as yet seriously shaken its position of supremacy.

But, paradoxically, the success of the Congress in maintaining so monolithic a unity may to some extent be due to its greatest failure — its failure to attract to its ranks the mass of politically-minded Muslims. For it has been kept together by the need for a united front not only against the British but, latterly, also against the Muslim demand for Pakistan and eventually against Pakistan itself. . . .

At the end of the war the British position in India seemed, on a superficial view, firmly entrenched and capable of meeting a serious challenge. The Viceroy held very wide powers, which wartime legislation had increased. His Executive Council consisted of his nominees, and was responsible neither formally to the Legislature nor informally to the political parties, but to him. Although the Indianisation of the administration had gone far, the two principal services — the Indian Civil Service and the Indian Police — still contained a considerable proportion of British officials, and the proportion was highest in the higher ranks. There were large British forces in India; and the Indian Army was British controlled and largely British officered. The Provincial Governors were all British, and in five out of the eleven Provinces they had been in control of the administration ever since the Congress Ministries resigned in October 1939. Lastly, all this vast organisation was under the ultimate direction of the Government in London. The British Parliament still had the final voice in Indian affairs.

The strength of this position was, however, more apparent than real. The essential factor was of course that Britain was pledged to give independence to India as soon as the main elements in the country could agree upon the broad lines of their future form of Government. . . .

With the war drawing to an end, ideas of liberation — national, racial and economic — had come into the air; and it was natural to feel that these must apply in India as elsewhere. Britain had had enough of war, and the maintenance in India of British troops for any considerable period and on a scale adequate to deal with a widespread revolt would have been stigmatised as a wanton misuse of British manpower and a waste of British lives; it would have been alleged that policy was being dictated by a small section who feared for their investments and trading interests. With a large part of the British public in this frame of mind, any Government which had come into armed conflict with Indian nationalism would have had to face an outcry against which it would have been hard put to defend itself. . . .

An armed collision would benefit no one. So, far from making the problem of India's future easier, it would only make her relations with Britain even more difficult, even more impregnated with bitterness. There was in addition the hard fact that Britain, impoverished by the war, could not afford a policy in India which would involve a further drain on her resources. Nor, whatever left-wing politicians might suspect, was there any economic motive strong enough to tempt her to stay in India, with the important proviso, of course, that she must if possible leave behind her conditions in which normal commercial operations would

not be made impossible by a breakdown of public order. The risk that a successor Government might take discriminatory action against British property was counterbalanced by the prospect that dealings between British and Indian business men would become friendlier when the political grounds for distrust were removed. Finally, the war had reversed the financial relations of the two countries. Britain's purchases of war supplies had been so vast that she was now no longer India's creditor but her debtor to the tune of £1,200 million. Hence there could no longer be any question of retaining some measure of control in order to ensure that an Indian Government fulfilled its liabilities.

Even if the British had not been pledged to hand over power, even if their own principles and their own difficulties had not predisposed them to do so, they might well have been influenced in the same direction by doubts as to the capacity of the existing administration to tackle the problems confronting the country. The dangers and difficulties in the economic field were well known. The population was increasing at the rate of some five million a year. The vast majority were illiterate peasants living on the barest margin of subsistence. And even more urgent than the raising of this miserable standard of living was the task of making it secure, lest the failure of the available food supplies to meet the needs of the mounting population should lead to famine on an unprecedented scale. Clearly therefore an immense effort was needed to ensure the fair distribution of essential goods, to develop agriculture and industry, and to improve communications, public health and education. It would be for Government to take the lead in planning and executing this drive for economic salvation, and to inspire the educated minority, from whom so much devoted service would be required, with a sense of high responsibility, even of mission. This would be a hard enough task for any Government; it could scarcely be undertaken by one which was responsible to an alien power, and whose every action evoked a torrent of criticism from nationalists who ascribed all their ills to the fact that their country had not achieved her freedom. . . .

The vast triangle of territory south of the Himalayan barrier is marked by few or no physical features which history has shown to afford natural frontiers. It is in fact a geographical unit, and this has been at the root of many of the troubles of the Indian sub-continent; inasmuch as it demands that for true security there must be a single authority capable of wielding power, or commanding loyalty, over substantially the whole area. Independence and partition forfeited this security, as the subsequent tension between the two new countries has amply proved. More, partition has involved very serious material disadvantages. For, whether or not nature intended this geographical unit to constitute also an economic unit, it is certain that the period of British rule, coinciding as it did with the development of modern communications, did much to weld it together economically. Partition, however, dictated as it was by political considerations, could recognise this only as a matter for regret. If the over-worked metaphor of vivisection is anywhere appropriate, it is to describe the effect of partition on the economic life of the former India. . . .

Yet it is hard to resist the conclusion that partition, however difficult and dangerous, was none the less inevitable. At least, if it had not always been so, it was surely the logical outcome of the events of the past forty years. The gradual demission of power by the British opened the way to a struggle for office, influence and authority; and the chief protagonists in the struggle became apparent when the Muslim renaissance, led by such men as Sir Syed Ahmed and Sir Muhammad Iqbal, clashed in full career with the Hindu renaissance inspired by Gandhi. These two movements had a double significance. First, they showed that the traditional cultures of India had had time to formulate their characteristic reactions to Western penetration. Secondly, they served to underline the fact that the Hindu and Muslim communities, though so largely of the same racial origins, had developed different and distinctive characters. The Muslims of India had passed the only really valid test of nationality — they were a nation because they profoundly believed themselves to be one. The best proof of this is the energy, enthusiasm and sense of mission with which the Indian Muslims, particularly those of the younger generation, have tackled the vast difficulties involved in building their new State. Thus has the two-nation theory evolved into the fact of the two nations of India and Pakistan. . . .

In Chapter I it has been argued that the situation at the end of the war was such as to demand that the transfer of power from British to Indian hands should be speedy and complete. The essence of statesmanship is surely to look at any given situation with a fresh and unprejudiced eye, to realise what it demands and act accordingly. Britain can fairly claim, then, that her withdrawal was in itself, and irrespective of the method adopted, an act of statesmanship. In retrospect it may seem that she merely took the obvious course, the line of least resistance. Yet there remain two striking facts. One is that her act of renunciation, however it may have been dictated by the hard facts of her postwar weakness, is one for which history affords no close precedent or analogy. The other is that the results which have followed from the pursuit of other policies by other European powers in their dealings with their Asian territories during recent years have been unfortunate for all concerned.

In the opening paragraph of this book three phases in the reaction of the Asiatic peoples to Western expansion were broadly distinguished. It was also implied that the story which was to be told concerned the second phase, since those to whom Britain handed over power were members of the educated middle class. If she had not acted so promptly, and if she had in consequence become involved in a war against the forces of nationalism, the outcome might well have been a rapid transition to the third phase. In other words, the victor in the struggle might have been neither of the ostensible protagonists, but the coalition of educated fanaticism and uneducated discontent which is comprehensively designated Communism. As it was, however, the new Governments of India and Pakistan were composed of men whose political philosophy had much in common with the liberal and social democracy of the West. British policy had therefore ensured that the leaders of the two new States should

be men who would talk to her in her own political language; but who, on the other hand, would be able to meet the formidable challenge of Communism in Asia in a way in which she herself could never have done. For no alien government, especially a government encumbered with all the multifarious commitments bequeathed them by their ancestors who had settled the country for the East India Company, could undertake the drastic reforms in land tenure and social custom which were required now that circumstances, ideas and feelings had changed with the times.

Nationalism, Communalism, and Partition

W. NORMAN BROWN

UNDER Britain India gained inner unity. It had a single rule everywhere unchallenged, which brought the whole subcontinent for the only time in its 2500 years of known history to the traditional ideal of living "under one royal parasol." This rule, again for the first time in the subcontinent's history, was strictly secular, favoring no religion. As united, India consisted in the nineteenth and twentieth centuries of many units, diverse in political character and often of mutually contradictory political aims, yet all were unified at the center. All owed common allegiance to the British Crown; all respected its representatives and its courts, police, army, and administration. Even the conflicting social groups in the population, which were never really homogenized but only shaken together in unstable union like oil and vinegar, were formally synthesized at the high-

est level of government and usually at that level were decently civil to one another....

The means used by Britain to hold India included a good deal of the "divide and rule" philosophy, whether by design, as nationalists used to charge, or because of the inner nature of imperialism operating automatically and unconsciously. Large regions, namely the Indian princely states, were allowed to lag politically behind the other parts, that is, the provinces comprising "British India," so that the two kinds of political units stood side by side physically but philosophically were in contradiction. Large social divisions of the population, especially the Muslims, were permitted and in effect encouraged to develop and express their already existing fear and hostility toward the Hindu majority and to stand apart as a divisive group....

The development of representative insti-

Reprinted by permission of the publishers from William Norman Brown, *The United States and India and Pakistan,* pp. 41–42, 106–113, 119–143, Cambridge, Mass.: Harvard University Press, Copyright, 1953, by The President and Fellows of Harvard College. (In one instance the excerpts have been rearranged from their order of appearance in the original work.)

tutions [in the twentieth century was] closely associated with the growth of nationalism. By successive demands Indians won concessions through the "Morley-Minto Reforms" of 1909, the "Montagu-Chelmsford Reforms" of 1919, the Constitution of 1935, and the Indian Independence Act of 1947. In the end Britain gave nationalism its full demand, not from generosity, as is frequently stated, so much as from recognizing that government of India as a British dependency was no longer either possible or desirable under the greatly changed conditions that followed World War II.

*　　*　　*

[On July 1, 1945] the British Labour Party swept the Churchill government out of office and in its turn attacked the problem of India. Churchill had been universally regarded in India as hostile to the country's political aspirations and general best interests, but members of the Labour Party had taken an attitude which Indians considered friendly. Most British spokesmen at that time seemed to accept the fact that India must quickly receive independence. One basic reason was Britain's sheer lack of choice. The British power had weakened conspicuously during the war, and it was doubtful if Britain could have afforded the effort to hold India by force. Another was a great public lack of interest in retaining India against her will. Britain was no longer going to receive as much economic profit from India as it had in the nineteenth century and the first decades of the twentieth. Instead India had become a great trouble, if not expense, through its continuous unrest, and in the British public there were many who thought the only answer was to relinquish responsibility at the first possible moment and let India go it alone.

This sentiment was confirmed by events in India during 1945–1946. These included anti-British riots in Calcutta, refusal of the Royal Air Force in India to obey orders in January 1946, and in February of the same year a mutiny of the Royal Indian Navy. Many members of Congress prepared themselves for an armed uprising, which, however, Sardar Vallabhbhai Patel succeeded in restraining. When in that same winter, the government brought to trial for treason the leaders of the Indian National Army, which the Japanese had organized from prisoners of war and used in Burma, popular feeling in their favor was so intense that the action had to be abandoned. In the circumstances, it was clear in Britain that her problem respecting India was merely to save for herself what she could as she withdrew and in the act of withdrawal to keep to a minimum the dislocation and damage bound to result because of the confused and bitter relations which had developed among Indian groups. . . .

*　　*　　*

The history of nationalism in India inspires two reflections, one concerning the British, the other concerning Indian nationalism. The first is that, with a moderate degree of political tact, Britain might have prevented the many serious disturbances that accompanied the march of India to independence, and might have succeeded in retaining it undivided as a Dominion. If in 1905 Bengal had from the first been divided according to linguistic boundaries rather than on the basis of greatest bureaucratic administrative efficiency; if in 1909 the enactment of the Morley-Minto Reforms had not been almost immediately followed by secret planning which led to the surprise removal of the capital from Calcutta to Delhi; if the reforms of 1919 had not had to fight their way through the brutality of the Amritsar massacre and military rule in the Punjab; if in 1927 the Simon Commission had been appointed with at least one Indian member; if in 1931 the repressive ordinances had not been issued at all, and especially if they had not come in close conjunction with the (to the nationalists) disappointing issue of the Second Round Table Conference; if in 1935 the new Constitution had not been framed with its uncompromising "safeguards" of British power and commerce — if at any of the junctures there had been more of conciliation and less of inflexibility, India might well have developed new political institutions through which unity with Britain could have been preserved.

The other reflection concerns the fact that Indian nationalism rose, grew, and expressed itself in the religio-social group of Hindus. It was not possible for this nationalism to win to itself the Muslims, adherents to another religio-centric manner of life, which in its way was just as intent upon survival as ever was Hinduism. It is true that the Indian National Congress, the organ of nationalism, never conceded itself to be the voice of Hindu India alone as distinguished from India as a whole. It adopted a secular program meant to produce a secular state; many of its most prominent leaders sincerely and consistently upheld secular aims in politics and eschewed religious and narrow communal aims. Among them were certain Muslims. But the stubborn fact remained that nationalism was a phenomenon of the Hindu community, and this community provided the strength and the direction of Congress, which, when it held power in 1937–1939, was not wise enough to win Muslim confidence. The rivalries already implicit in the situation were exacerbated by the communal activities of the Hindu Mahasabha, which frankly advocated violence against Muslims and goaded Congress as far as it could to communal action. The masses of each community, and more narrowly, the middle classes, which were those fostering political activity, never forgot the contrasts and antipathies of Hinduism and Islam. Hence they could not cross the barrier of communalism and press ahead in common effort to solve the problems posed before their country by the conditions of the mid-twentieth-century world.

* * *

When on August 15, 1947 India was simultaneously given self-government and partitioned into two nations, the western world viewed the gain of independence as the more dramatic of the two changes and the more newsworthy. For it ended the epoch of British political rule, thereby diminishing Britain's world power, and at the same time raised India from her unflattering status as the world's greatest colony. But whatever any distant nations in the West thought of developments, the attainment of full self-rule was neither the more sudden nor the more significant for the subcontinent. Rather, those qualities lay with partition. Self-rule had been in sight for years. But partition was a recent thing. It had not been advocated by a political party until 1940, and then it had appeared unrealistic, a mirage, promoted for propaganda and bargaining purposes but never likely to be realized. Very quickly, however, in 1942 when the Cripps offer was made, it acquired a semblance of reality, yet still no certainty. As late as May 1946, at the time of the Cabinet Mission, partition seemed near to death. Not until June 3, 1947, just over ten weeks before the fateful day itself, did it become a certainty, and when it was effected, it was done with such celerity that there was no time to devise adequate plans for a smooth division, to say nothing of creating the necessary machinery for accomplishing it.

Yet the importance of partition was fundamental. It struck the subcontinent where it lived. It disrupted its new economy, its communications, its administration. It weakened its defense. It divided it into mutually antipathetic and suspicious nations, with a clashing cultural discord inherited from a long past, that only briefly and temporarily had been muted during the eighteenth century and had been steadily rising during the nineteenth and twentieth.

Partition was a direct result of communalism. This is the term given in India and Pakistan to the sense of insecurity which any community feels and the accompanying action it takes to protect itself and further its own interests. It is applied in different localities to groups differentiated by religion, language, region, historical origin, occupation. That is, it has in different areas marked off Hindus, Muslims, Sikhs, Parsis, Christians; speakers of Hindi, Bengali, Marathi, Telugu, and other languages; Mundas, Dravidians, Aryans, Anglo-Indians; agriculturists, jute factory owners, industrial workers. Because a number of these various communities were recognized in British India by separate political constituencies, communalism has had a peculiarly aggravated form in the subcontinent. It is above all applied to the ill-feeling existing in Hindu-Muslim relationships. The Muslims dislike the beliefs and ways of the Hindus, distrust them, and as a minority have feared for their treatment if they should have to live in a state where the Hindu majority had acceded to power. The Hindus in their turn dislike the ways of the Muslims, and, though a majority, have feared the rise to power of the Muslims under whom they experienced centuries of oppression. Before partition the Hindu-Muslim communal hostility was an internal problem of the single undivided India; after partition it became a source of international issues between the two new nations and has helped materially to produce a danger of war. It is the subcontinent's most corrosive inheritance from the past.

*   *   *

Before the agitation that led to partition, in trade unions and peasant groups members of the two communities had often learned to work in cooperation. Among the ruling princes, the antipathy might be suppressed or ignored. It was the middle classes, economically ambitious, that were the chief field in which it appeared. They attached the most value to strict religious dogma; at the same time the system of communal legislative representation and political appointment produced in them heated rivalry and permanent tension, which they communicated on opportunity to the masses. Thereupon on some minor provocation, Muslim mullahs, Hindu priests, or fanatic laymen of either community might by raising the Muslim cry of Din ("The Religion") or the Hindu charge of sacrilege, precipitate a riot.

Several aspects of Hindu-Muslim relations, which showed some degree of cultural assimilation, used to give proponents of the one-nation theory some ground for hope that at a future time, however remote, the hostility might disappear. The one which leaders of the Indian National Congress most often used to stress is the fact that Hindus and Muslims in each locality of India and Pakistan belong to the same racial and ethnic stock. Islam spread in India by conversion rather than by immigration. And conversions were made not so much by force, though force was often used and the memory is bitter in Hindus, as by missionary enterprise among the lowest in the Hindu social and economic scale, who found relief from many disabilities in accepting Islam. In every part of India and Pakistan Hindus and Muslims are alike physically; they can be distinguished only by externals, such as dress, treatment of facial and head hair, sectarian markings, customs of eating, drinking, or other. Moreover, in every locality both parts of the population use a common speech.

Socially, too, there has been occasional assimilation of the two groups, for example, in using similar wedding ceremonies and in sharing each other's religious festivals. Muslim dress has affected, though seldom completely supplanted, native Hindu middle-class costume. The Muslim habit of secluding women became a local practice of those Hindus who could afford it. Caste, though contrary to Muslim doctrine, nevertheless exists in a number of Muslim groups, which could not entirely rid themselves of caste practices when accepting conversion. . . .

Finally, the two communities have much of common history. Rulers of one faith have frequently made alliances with rulers of the other against rulers of their own faith. Muslim rulers have often used Hindus as civil administrators and generals, and Hindus have done the same with Muslims. During the British period in India the hereditary rulers of each group were deprived of their political power by the intruding Europeans, and the masses of both suffered economically as their agrarian system was revolutionized and their handicrafts put in competition with western machine industry. The two communities, on high and low levels alike, had a measure of joint interest in gaining self-rule.

The various religious and other cultural differences defined the two communities and produced their primary misunderstandings. But these might have been overlaid and become negligible in their effect upon national life if they had not been supplemented by economic disparities and political rivalries. It happened that in several large areas there was a religious dichotomy of landlords or moneylenders and peasantry. The one would be Muslim, the other Hindu. Thus, in the United Provinces (now Uttar Pradesh), where the peasantry was Hindu, there was a large class of Muslim landholders, called taluqdars. The reverse situation existed in parts of Bengal and the Punjab, where the Muslim peasantry paid rent to Hindu landlords or interest to Hindu moneylenders. In such situations the clash between economic classes was sure to become identified with religious difference.

There was also rivalry between the Hindu and Muslim middle classes created in part by an accident of geography. Because the Muslims had entered India from the northwest and were chiefly concentrated in the north and away from the seaports where the British entered and conducted most of their activities, it was the Hindus, living in and near those parts, who first profited economically from British commerce and first took advantage of the new western education. They became the agents to spread this education, and this fact, too, operated to the Muslim disadvantage and discontent. In Bengal Muslims avoided the learning which was brought by Western unbelievers and propagated by Hindu idolaters. Further, when the British reorganized the system of land tenure, the new

landlords under the British were Hindus, who had previously been only tax farmers under the Muslim regime. The old Muslim upper classes remained as landowners in their own areas, but the newly appointed Hindus became their upstart rivals as a prestige group and partly displaced them and reduced their numbers.

It was also the Hindus who developed the new bourgeoisie. By the time of the Indian Mutiny in 1857 the Muslim community had only a small middle class against the relatively large Hindu professional, clerical, and commercial groups. This condition persisted down to the time of partition. It was said that in East Bengal, now part of Pakistan, 80 per cent of trade and commerce was in Hindu hands. Moneylenders were almost all Hindus, and the jute business, which is the major industry of East Bengal, was also Hindu. Similarly, about 90 per cent of the professional classes were Hindu. This situation has altered under Pakistan. It was also the Hindus (and Parsis) who became the new industrialists, not the Muslims, most of whose leaders continued to be of the old landholder class.

There was another situation in the nineteenth century operating to Muslim disadvantage. When the Indian Mutiny occurred it was considered by the British to be a responsibility of the Muslims. Most of the Indian Princes involved were Muslim, and the head of a freed India, as the Mutiny would have made it, was to be the titular Mughal emperor in Delhi, around whose shadowy figure the mutineers had assembled their forces. Because of this fact, the British, after quelling the Mutiny, laid the heavier part of the penalty upon the Muslims. It was approximately a decade later before they lifted this discrimination.

During the second half of the nineteenth century the Muslim community contained the larger part of India's dispossessed and unhappy great. It no longer had the political supremacy enjoyed under the Mughals, whose might had been destroyed by the Hindu Marathas and the Christian British, both of them infidels. The greater number of government posts open to Indians fell to Hindus, and the profits of business were theirs as well. By the time the century was three-quarters past, the old Muslim landlords, who held their position under government title, were still in possession of large sections of Bengal, Bihar, Orissa, and the United Provinces, but in other respects Hindus had the better status. It was inevitable that this situation should produce intercommunity middle-class jealousy. . . .

The growth of Indian nationalism during the twentieth century brought an accompanying increase in the number and intensity of intercommunal riots and took the clash between Muslims and Hindus out of religion and economics into politics. Intercommunity relations grew critical in 1905 over the partition of Bengal, which became a polemical issue of Hindu versus Muslim. The Muslims correctly foresaw that the Hindus might get the partition reversed — as it was in 1911 — and to prevent the reversal as well as generally to advance Muslim interests, some of their leaders in 1906, with the blessing of the Viceroy Lord Minto, organized the Muslim League (often called "the League"). Among its specific aims one was to secure for Muslims a due share of government posts. Another was to give the Muslim community a political organization; for it was apparent that India would soon be granted the right to elect some of the members of the provincial councils — the right was later defined in the Indian Councils Act ("Morley-Minto Reforms") of 1909.

It was the Morley-Minto Reforms that inaugurated modern Indian political communalism. In giving the country a limited form of representation in provincial Legislative Councils these reforms introduced the principle of "communal representation" through separate electorates and weightage of representation for minorities. By that system legislative seats and political appointments were apportioned among the general constituency and a number of special constituencies, most of which were defined along communal lines. One of these consisted of Muslims, who had their own representatives, for whom only Muslims voted. The general constituency was the non-Muslim population and corresponded closely with the Hindu community.

When the system of separate representation and separate electorates was introduced, its sponsors stated that it was meant to solve the communal problem; instead it only intensified it. From time to time every minority increased its demands for weightage in representation and appointments. The general constituency, speaking through Congress, resisted these demands, but was compelled to concede more and more. The chief dispute was always with the Muslims. In the two successive constitutions granted India after the Morley-Minto Reforms, namely those of 1919 and 1935, the principle of communal representation was extended instead of curtailed, and it thus became the most poisonous single feature of Indian politics in this century. . . .

The Muslims had a genuine alarm that their community might not be able to maintain itself against the Hindu, which during the millennia of history has quietly absorbed other rivals. They feared that their faith might perish in the land, and they and their descendants be reduced economically and socially. Their attention was kept focused on the communal quarrel; their leaders were slow in evolving a social or economic program for the community; they offered little more hope than vague benefits to be derived from establishing a religiously motivated state. This was the meaning Muslims gave to nationalism, and generally they preferred an India under Britain to a free India which might be dominated by the Hindus. Political activity they saw as their rivals' most potent weapon for their oppression; they made it, therefore, their own chief weapon for community protection.

In the 1940's the Indian Muslim community acquired the goal of a national Muslim state to be created by the partition of India into two separate nations, one Muslim, the other Hindu. The proposed

Muslim state was popularly called Pakistan. The Muslim League at a meeting in Lahore, on March 23, 1940, formally adopted the goal but did not then give the proposed state a name. . . .

There were from the beginning certain obvious and weighty objections to dividing India into two nations. First, the Hindu-Muslim communal problem, which the creation of Pakistan was to solve, clearly would still exist. In Hindustan there would be a Muslim minority and in Pakistan there would be non-Muslim minorities, which were already protesting. The Sikhs, for example, who lived chiefly in the eastern Punjab, were uncompromisingly opposed to Pakistan or anything that looked like it. Again, western Bengal, containing India's premier city, Calcutta, was predominantly Hindu. Jinnah [the president of the Muslim League] indicated at various times that provincial boundary lines might be redrawn, but he and the League were never reconciled to any redrawing that would entail, as was nevertheless inevitable, the loss of Calcutta.

Second, there were certain administrative and economic disadvantages sure to result from Pakistan. Operation of the railroads, postal and telegraph services, and probably some other departments of national life, which were organized on an all-India basis, would be inefficient in a divided subcontinent. Economically, the proposed Pakistan would contain some weak members: Baluchistan and the North-West Frontier regularly required financial assistance from the rest of India. Division could not fail to hinder seriously the exchange of agricultural products and impair industrial development. It was sure, at the minimum, to produce tariffs and customs barriers.

Third, the two parts of the proposed Pakistan would be separated from each other by a gap of 700 miles, across which they could communicate only by courtesy of the proposed "Hindustan." When partition was effected, the area of Pakistan was lessened and the gap became a thousand miles. Finally, the princely Indian States would have to adjust themselves to two independent nations, instead of one. These disadvantages were so certain, so clearly pointed out, so much calculated to affect Muslims as well as Hindus, that they seemed to most foreign observers to forbid creation of Pakistan. . . .

During the first three or four years after the Muslim League formally adopted Pakistan as its goal (1940), the vogue of the idea in the Muslim community as a whole was restricted. A number of Muslim parties were relatively indifferent to it; some others were directly opposed. The latter were not only the anti-communalist Muslim members of the Indian National Congress, who were organized as a subparty called the Nationalist Muslim Party, but also other Muslim groups. . . . Most of these bodies either never were effective in politics or by 1946 had lost the effectiveness they once had. The Nationalist Muslims, for example, won only 11 seats against the League's total of 426 in the 1946 provincial elections; the Jamiat-al-Ulama won only 5; the Momins 5, the Ahrars 1.

One group which was always opposed to Pakistan and was the only really strong Muslim organization combating it, was that of the Khuda-i-Khidmatgar ("Servants of God"), the so-called "Red Shirts" of the North-West Frontier Province. This was a group closely affiliated to the Congress; its leader, Abdul Ghaffar Khan, was deeply influenced by Gandhi's teaching and practice of non-violence and introduced similar doctrine and methods among his Pathan followers in resisting the Government of India. In the 1946 elections this group won 19 of the 34 seats reserved for Muslims in the North-West Frontier Province; the League won the other 15. The Red Shirts' seats together with the nine general seats and two of the three Sikh seats gave them control of the province, and Abdul Ghaffar Khan's brother, Doctor Khan Sahib, became premier of the province.

For several years after the League adopted Pakistan, the chief support for it came, not from the Muslim provinces

which were expected to constitute the
Muslim state, but from Muslims in provinces that were not to be included. It was
opposed in Assam as well as in the North-
West Frontier Province. In the Punjab,
Bengal, and Sind the support was luke-
warm and the opposition too strong for the
League and Jinnah to overcome until after
the Churchill government in 1942–1945
had confined the leaders of Congress and
so crippled it. The premiers of those three
provinces were at first all outside the
League. It was the United Provinces (now
Uttar Pradesh) and other regions where
the Muslims were numerically inferior to
the Hindus and therefore apprehensive that
gave Pakistan its early strength.

After the Churchill government in 1942
sent Sir Stafford Cripps to India with constitutional proposals that would have made
Pakistan possible, the impression got around
among Muslims that the British, who after
all had the power, felt that the proposal for
Pakistan was reasonable and should be
granted – or, at least, that the Churchill
government was supporting it. The Cripps
offer went a long way toward making the
League inflexible on Pakistan.

*   *   *

The War Cabinet's proposals, if they had
been meant to confuse the Indian political
situation, could hardly have been more
skillfully framed. They offered independence on terms liable to shatter India into
many parts. Congress considered the offer
illusory and refused it. The proffer of something which Churchill, who was well-
informed on the Indian situation and at the
same time a most astute politician, must
have known was unrealistic and would be
rejected, led to frustration of the nationalists. The proposals suddenly transformed
the Muslim League program of Pakistan
from a bargaining weapon meant to wring
concessions from the Congress into a realiz-
able goal, and must be considered the most
important single step toward the 1947
partition.

*   *   *

Various compromise solutions of the
Pakistan issue were proposed during the
years 1940–1946. The common element in
all was decentralization of government. . . .

In promoting Pakistan, however, the
Muslim League was inflexible and would
accept no compromise. From the time of
the War Cabinet's offer in 1942, during the
remaining war years, the prestige of the
Muslim League as promoter of Pakistan
steadily increased. At the same time the
strength of the Indian National Congress was declining under the attack of
Churchill's government, which outlawed
both the All-India and the provincial Congress organizations, confined its leaders, and
seemed bent on destroying the Congress as
a political force. The 1945–1946 elections
in India, which the League fought on the
sole issue of Pakistan, showed the growth
of its power. Though in the last previous
elections (1937) for the provincial assemblies, the Muslim League had been able
to win but 104 seats out of the 482 consti-
tutionally reserved for and elected only by
the Muslim community, in 1946 it won
412. The League also won 14 other seats,
including 9 of the 10 reserved for Muslim
women; in 1937 it had won only 5 other
seats. Again, in the elections to the Central
Legislative Assembly, the League won all
the 30 seats reserved for the Muslim
constituency.

Confirmed then by this solid support,
the League and Jinnah demanded Pakistan
as an unalterable condition precedent to
any further steps leading to a solution of
the constitutional problem. The Indian
National Congress refused to accept this,
though it was willing to move from its
stand in favor of a strong closely knit central government to one with very much
limited powers.

The climax was now not far distant. In
March 1946 the British Labour Government sent out a three-man Cabinet Mission (including Cripps) to try to solve the
constitutional problem, and on May 16,
1946, the Mission's plan was read in the
House of Commons by Prime Minister

Attlee as a White Paper. The Cabinet Mission, though rejecting the Pakistan demand in its full and complete form, made extensive concessions to it. . . .

To carry on government until a Constituent Assembly could be elected, the Mission's plan provided for the appointment of an Interim Cabinet, which was to be a coalition and have "the support of the major political parties."

The whole plan in the end failed and as it was failing the tense relations between the two communities snapped strand by strand. The League demanded parity with Congress in the Interim Government (five portfolios each out of a total of twelve) and the sole right to nominate any Muslim. Congress would allow only five portfolios to the League against six to itself, feeling that in view of its greater strength parity would be unfair — it held 56 seats in the Central Legislative Assembly against the League's 30, and in the provincial legislatures held more than twice as many. Nor would it relinquish the right to nominate a Muslim, since it was not a communal body, as was the League, and was not going to be jockeyed into appearing as one. The League at first boycotted the Interim Government, but afterwards, when such a government took office (September 2) with its membership nominated by Congress, it agreed to enter (October 12), not having won its points. This Government, however, operated without teamwork, the members apparently never meeting in full session but transacting most of their Cabinet business by correspondence.

In respect to the Constituent Assembly which was to frame India's new Constitution, the League refused to cooperate. Jawaharlal Nehru, President of the Congress, had made an indiscreet statement on July 10, 1946, "The big probability is that there will be no grouping." He had indicated that the arrangement of provinces in sections for the Constituent Assembly, as provided in the Cabinet Mission's plan, was unacceptable to two provinces (Assam and the North-West Frontier Province), then controlled by Congress but included in the Muslim sections, and would therefore be abrogated by them as soon as the sections should meet, instead of at the later time indicated in the plan. The League said that such statements showed that Congress had been insincere in accepting the plan.

When the announcement was made that a government would be formed even without the League's cooperation, the League endeavored to arouse the Muslim community. Jinnah said, "Goodbye to constitutional methods and constitutionalism," and the League adopted a resolution directing "the Working Committee to prepare forthwith a programme of direct action . . . and to organize the Muslims for the coming struggle to be launched as and when necessary." It named August 16 as "Direct Action Day," calling for demonstrations, which it said should be non-violent. But Bengal and Bihar had had almost continuous riots throughout 1946, and that day and several following were marked by the bloodiest communal rioting in Calcutta which India had yet known. Bengal had a Muslim Government and the premier, H. S. Suhrawardy, was afterwards accused of complicity. In the weeks following there were communal riots in Bombay and many other cities, and the disturbances in Bihar against Muslims and in eastern Bengal against Hindus broke out again in the most extreme form. The district of Noakhali in Bengal, where Muslims outnumbered Hindus four or five to one, was pacified only when Gandhi made a tour through it. These various disturbances seemed like possible opening moves in the civil war which Jinnah had prophesied would be inevitable if India were given self-government without the accompanying award of Pakistan.

The dispute between Congress and the League over the grouping of provinces in the Constituent Assembly continued uninterruptedly and inconclusively through the summer and autumn. . . .

In the constantly deteriorating situation the Labour Government now made a desperate — but not yet its most desperate —

effort to stop the bloody dispute. Mr. Attlee announced on February 20, 1947 that by June 1948 at the latest the British Government would grant full self-government to British India in one of three ways: either to British India as a unit, or to existing provincial governments, or in some other way that would be "in the best interests of the Indian people." At the same time Earl Mountbatten of Burma was appointed Viceroy in place of Lord Wavell.

When Lord Mountbatten got to India, he made a quick examination of the situation, noted statements of Congress leaders (Nehru, Rajendra Prasad) showing them receptive to partition as a means of ending the bloodshed, found Jinnah aware that he would have to accept a smaller Pakistan than he had been demanding, and discovered the Sikhs ready to concede division of the Punjab. He then returned to London, where he recommended a drastic course of action which was promptly accepted. On June 3, the British Government outlined a plan for partitioning India and the next day announced that the appointed day for independence and partition would be August 15. In July, Parliament passed the Indian Independence Act by which India was divided into two independent nations, each with full Dominion Status, while the Indian States were left free to accede to whichever they wished. . . .

Everything had to be done with the greatest haste. As Lord Mountbatten put it: it had taken three years to separate Burma from India, two years to separate Sind from Bombay, and two years to separate Orissa from Bihar, but only two and a half months were taken to divide all India in two. The result was action without adequate preparation.

The two new nations started off badly. In the capitals great crowds celebrated the independence — in Karachi with the slogan "Long live Pakistan" (*pakistan zindabad*); in Delhi with "Victory to India" (*jay hind*). But this was only a minute fraction of the total response, which was opposite, savage, and appalling. For the violence that now

occurred was colossal, beyond all that Indian, Pakistani, or British officials had feared. It had begun before August 15. In West Punjab and the North-West Frontier, Muslims murdered Sikhs and Hindus; in East Punjab and the Sikh states, Sikhs and Hindus murdered Muslims. In parts of the United Provinces Hindus and Muslims murdered each other. In the border regions of Jammu and Kashmir Sikhs crossed as refugees from West Pakistan to spread violence. Peaceful villages suddenly became two hostile camps, one portion of the population trying to exterminate the other. In the cities, especially in Lahore and Delhi, terrorism was in control. Houses were fired, looting went unchallenged, women were kidnapped, massacre took place on the main highways. The leaders of neither side could control the situation. Pakistanis charged that the Sikhs and the armed and drilled Rashtriya Swayamsevak Sangh [a militant Hindu organization — ED.] operated by plan in well-directed organization, as apparently they did; the further charges that high Indian officials abetted them have not been substantiated. Indians charged that Pakistani troops detailed to guard Sikhs and Hindus instead took part in the slaughter. The number of deaths by direct violence is unknown; claims run up to a million. Various Americans and British working at relief in the affected areas at the time have guessed — and they have claimed to do no more than guess — that it was over 100,000, possibly at the outside 200,000. Besides the deaths by violence there were others from disease, hunger, exposure, for floods came at this time, too. The total may have come close to half a million. For weeks there were wide areas where the situation was little short of anarchic. In Bengal, killings were fewer, partly because Gandhi exercised a check there.

A corollary of the violence was mass migration. Fearful Hindus and Sikhs left Western Punjab, and Muslims left East Punjab and nearby regions of the United Provinces. There is probably not a Sikh (except for members of some quietistic sects in Sind) left today in Western Pakistan, and few Hindus. Many Muslims left India. The migration extended over months. In Bengal migrations have continued down to the present. The total number of migrants both ways in all parts of the subcontinent is set down at 12,000,000; if the two governments' claims are added it comes to a couple of million more. This is the greatest movement of population known to history.

The immediate responsibility for the tragedies occurring at the time of partition must be laid to Hindu-Muslim communal antipathy, fomented by the Muslim League, the Hindu Mahasabha, and many individuals not belonging to either organization but animated by the communal spirit. But Indian National Congress shortsightedness and Muslim League intransigence had set the stage, while the British, by their political policies for fifty years, had augmented the communal mistrust. At the last moment the British were also unequal to the double demand of abrogating power and at the same time protecting those who had been subject to it.

Asia and Western Dominance

K. M. PANIKKAR

THE period of maritime authority over Asia, beginning with Vasco da Gama's arrival and ending with the departure of the Western fleets from their bases on the Asian continent, covers an epoch of the highest significance to human development. The changes it directly brought about and the forces it generated in the countries of Asia in contact with Europe for a period of 450 years, and subjected to Western domination for over a century, have effected a transformation which touches practically every aspect of life in these countries.

Though it is impossible to anticipate what Asia will make of these influences in the future, and how the different Asian countries will transmute the experiences, ideas and institutions in the crucible of their racial characteristics, history and social tradition, there is no gainsaying the fact that the massiveness of the changes that have already taken place, the upsurges that have modified their outlook, involve a qualitative break with the past which justly entitles the changes to be described as revolutionary. The period of European control of the States of Asia is a dividing line in their history, for both by resistance and by adaptation they have had to call forth new vitality and consciously adapt themselves to new ideas by which alone they were able gradually to recover their independence and strength. . . .

If by an Act of God the relations of Europe with Asia had ceased all of a sudden in 1748, little would have been left to show for two and a half centuries of furious activity. Even in India, there would have only been a few ruined forts on unfrequented coasts, some churches erected also in coastal areas by the Portuguese, a small community of half-castes, regretting the days when they were people of prestige —

From K. M. Panikkar, *Asia and Western Dominance: A Survey of the Vasco Da Gama Epoch of Asian History, 1498–1945* (London, 1959), pp. 313, 315–320, 323–332. By permission of George Allen & Unwin, Ltd.

hardly anything more. In the trading period, 1610–1758, Europe influenced Asia but little.

In the period of conquest (1750–1857), however, the situation began to change. Asian leaders began to feel that the strangers had become a menace and had to be taken seriously. It is not surprising that the first serious interest that the Asian leaders began to show was in cannon-making, army organization and military equipment. But apart from this justifiable curiosity in respect of military matters shown by a few people in power, there were others who were interested in the intellectual and spiritual strength of the European nations. Ram Mohan Roy and his school in India and the Rangakusha school in Japan are examples of this changing attitude towards Europe. Citizen Tipoo as a member of the Jacobin Club of Seringapatam, Ram Mohan Roy in correspondence with the leaders of the Enlightenment in Europe, and public meetings in Calcutta to congratulate the liberal revolutionaries in Spain were symptoms of an intellectual awakening and a sense of world-community which was dawning on Asia.

The most significant single factor which changed the intellectual relationship of Europe and Asia was the French Revolution. Few people today realize the immense influence of the French Revolution outside Europe. Negroes in Haiti, Tipoo in Mysore, Dutch radicals in Indonesia, all felt the ripples of this movement. The reforms of Dandaels in Java were a direct result of it. Wellesley's aggressive policy leading to the conquest and annexation of large areas of India was one of its indirect consequences, for it was fear of the revolutionary French that provided the main motive of his policy of conquest. But it is not in this sense that the doctrines of the French Revolution — "liberty, equality and fraternity" — came to have a pervading influence on Asia. As a revolution the developments in France had but little immediate influence on the Asian people. In the period that followed the Napoleonic experiment, the doctrines of the Revolution had become the common inheritance of European liberalism. Modified and made respectable by the reformers in the period immediately following the Napoleonic era, they became the mental background of European statesmen. Education could no longer be neglected in the possessions of European nations. Codes of modern law had to be provided; and even the Dutch had to pay lip service to the interests of the Indonesians when they recovered the lost colony of Java. Slowly a liberal tradition penetrated the policies of European nations.

Not only did the French revolutionary doctrines become in due course an influence on European thought in relation to the East, but they provided the Asian peoples with their first political ideology. Indian writings of the first period of nationalism hark back to the principles of this school. Ram Mohan Roy and his followers, petitioning for the abolition of *Suttee,* for education in English, for greater freedom for women, though they quote from Hindu scriptures in justification of their reforms, are really thinking in terms of Rousseau, watered down to meet Indian conditions. European inspiration of the Asian reform movements of the first half of the nineteenth century cannot be denied.

The nineteenth century witnessed the apogee of capitalism in Europe. That this was in a large measure due to Europe's exploitation of Asian resources is now accepted by historians. As Hobson, the historian of Imperialism, observes: "The exploitation of other portions of the world, through military plunder, unequal trade and forced labour, has been the one great indispensable condition in the growth of European capitalism." It is the riches of Asian trade (and American) flowing to Europe that enabled the great industrial revolution to take place in England. But with the establishment of capitalism as the dominant economic structure of the colonizing nations, an immense and far-reaching change took place in the relations of the

West with Asia. In the eighteenth century, conquest was for the purpose of trade. In the area you conquered, you excluded other nations, bought at the cheapest price, organized production by forced labour to suit your requirements, and transferred the profits to the mother country. In the nineteenth century conquest was not for trade but for investment. Tea plantations and railway construction became major interests in Britain's connection with India. Vast sums were invested in India for building railways. "Of the loans for Indian Railways," says an English writer, "about one-third went to pay the home charges in London, something under one-third was spent on wages and administrative expenses, largely paid to English engineers, and something over one-third on British rails and engines and in paying British ships to bring them to India."

The third phase of European relations with Asia, which begins with the middle of the nineteenth century, is the period of imperialism in the true sense of the word. The transformation is completed earliest in India, which provides the pattern for the rest, for the Dutch in Indonesia, for the French in Indo-China, for all the nations in respect of China. The imperialist relationship, involving large-scale capital investment, had the result of importing into Asia advanced technical skills and scientific knowledge. Railway construction, which was the main field of capital investment, required the importation of engineers. Rivers had to be spanned, tunnels had to be built, and the lines, once constructed, had to be maintained. Imported technical skill, except at the highest levels, became too costly, and as a result engineering colleges and schools became unavoidable. The spread of technical knowledge in the East, of which this is merely an example, was a necessary result of capital investment. It was not possible to keep Asian nations out of this knowledge, for returns on capital depended on finding technical skill locally. In regard to industry also, a similar movement became noticeable. European indus-tries established in Calcutta, Bombay and Shanghai had to depend, at least in their lower levels, on locally trained personnel. With the advancement of knowledge among local populations it became impossible to prevent Asian capital from encroaching on European industrial monopolies. In India, cotton mills began to spring up in Bombay and Ahmedabad. In Shanghai, which had become practically a European city, Chinese industrialists found no difficulty in setting up factories in imitation of European models. . . . Thus, in its primary aspect, imperialism as an export of capital carried into Asia the seeds of its own destruction.

In its second aspect, that is territorial expansion for providing areas for exploitation, European imperialism in the nineteenth century, under the humanitarian impulses of the liberal movement, embarked on a policy of education, welfare schemes and even political training. Direct administration of vast populations naturally created new interests. The administrative authorities had no direct connection with or interest in trade, the officers being, at least according to English tradition, recruited from the middle classes with public school training. So in India, and to some extent in Indonesia, a contradiction developed within the structure of imperialism in which the administrative authorities were inclined to emphasize the welfare aspect of their work, while the commercial interests still considered the territories as areas for exploitation. The conflict between the two views came out into the open in India in the controversy on the Ilbert Bill[1] and in the successive movements to resist political reforms, of which the inspiration and the leadership lay always with big business. . . . In fact political authority, combined with the humanitarian ideals of the era of peace, brought a sense of responsibility towards

[1] A measure proposed in 1883 which would have made possible the trial of Englishmen in India before Indian judges; because of the protest aroused by the Bill, it was withdrawn in favor of a more limited measure. [Editor's note]

"the backward peoples." No danger to the supremacy of Europe was suspected as being inherent in this development, for even at the end of the nineteenth century the Europeans — even the most progressive among them — were convinced that their superiority was divinely ordained and was safe at least for centuries to come. The idea that the Chinese, weak, immobilized and without industrial potential, could stand up and fight the European within a measurable time, or that Indians could compete with the British in trade or industry, or that the hundreds of Indonesian islands could be united in opposition to the Dutch, would have sounded ludicrous to a European in the Augustan age of imperialism. Therefore the humanitarian ideal of educating the Asian people and of encouraging them to develop at least those skills which were necessary for the more effective discharge of the white man's mission, was pursued without any sense of fear.

Also, the complexities of direct administration of vast areas like India and Indonesia made it necessary to develop a large body of indigenous administrative personnel. In the period of trade there was no such necessity. In the period of imperialism this was unavoidable.

The apparatus of modern States, run largely by local talent, had to be built up, providing the Asian peoples both with administrative training and with knowledge and understanding of the mechanism of modern government. This is particularly important, for one of the main differences between the earlier periods of history and the political systems that developed in the nineteenth and twentieth centuries lay in the vast administrative systems which touched every aspect of life which the State organizations of the nineteenth and twentieth centuries represented. In the eighteenth century, neither in Europe nor in Asia was there a government which was also an administration in the present-day sense. In the latter half of the nineteenth century European countries, having had to deal with more and more complex problems

of industry, commerce, social and economic welfare, organized the vast mechanism of modern administration, which neither Frederick the Great nor Napoleon could have conceived, and which earlier political thought would have resisted bitterly as encroachments on liberty.

The Asian State-systems, though essentially bureaucratic and therefore "administrative" and not political, were, however, limited to land administration and defence. The administrative system which the Crown developed in India and which every colonial administration felt compelled to develop in its territory, not only provided the first conception of the modern State to the Asian mind, but equipped it with the mechanism necessary to realize it in time....

The third aspect of territorial expansion — of the era of imperialism — was the popular sentiment of responsibility for "moral wellbeing" which found its most characteristic expression in the missionary work. The conscience of the people, especially of the Protestant countries, was aroused by the fact that in the areas directly governed by them or under their influence hundreds of millions lived and died without the chance of salvation. . . . Thousands of serious-minded, pious men . . . devoted themselves to the cause of evangelization and spent their lives in the different countries of Asia. Though the results of their religious activities were negligible and often led only to reactions which they least expected, their interest in the life and wellbeing of the common people, and their efforts to break down the barrier of race, had the benefit of bringing the West nearer to Asia. Also, their educational and medical work in the interior of India, China and Burma had far-reaching consequences.

It is necessary to emphasize that the contact between the peoples of the East with Europeans began really only in the era of imperialism. In the 300 and odd years that preceded it (from 1498 to 1858) this contact was limited, even in India, to narrow circles, and had not penetrated even into the ruling classes. With direct administration, development of educational systems, exploitation instead of trade, the contact gradually extended to different levels. Slowly Asian youths began to find their way to European seats of learning. . . . The first impulse which took young Indians across the seas was not to probe the mysteries of European life, but the more material consideration of a chance to compete in the Civil Service examinations. But soon this movement assumed immense proportions, and a large proportion of the students who went to Europe were dedicated to the study of such subjects as engineering, medicine, forestry, geology and chemistry apart, of course, from law and social sciences. . . .

The essential point for our purpose is that in every one of the countries of Asia, the leadership in the movement which ultimately displaced European supremacy belonged to those who had been trained by the West under the aegis of imperialism. Not only Mahatma Gandhi and Jawaharlal Nehru, but the founders of the Indian National Congress and the successive generations of Congress leaders were trained in the West. . . .

There is a view generally held by many European writers that the changes brought about in Asia by the contact with Europe are superficial and will, with the disappearance of European political authority, cease to count as time goes on. They point out that the vast masses in India, China, Indonesia and even Japan have remained unaffected by the changes in their countries, and that the penetration of Western ideas has been confined to limited classes: that the great Oriental religions have held firm under assault, that the life in the East in spite of the appearance of great change moves in the familiar old grooves. The view is therefore advanced that with the elimination of European political authority Asia will revert to type and the Western influence will be gradually swept away by the indigenous ways of life.

This point of view would seem to be based on a superficial reading of history. Though the Hindus, the Chinese and the Japanese liked to believe that their own cultures were superior they could not deny either the superiority of Western knowledge or the greater strength – though not the stability – of the European social and economic organization. They were convinced, after a short period of intoxication, that their own religious and moral systems were superior but they had ample proofs to satisfy them that Europe was intellectually centuries ahead of them. European learning, therefore, earned the respect of all Asians during a whole century and, what is more, European social and economic organization provided a norm which, in part, they accepted enthusiastically and, in part, was forced upon them by world conditions. This had never happened before, at least in the history of India and China. Five hundred years of Muslim authority in North India had not forced the Hindus to change their social ideas in regard to caste and untouchability – in fact, it had strengthened them. . . . Today, however, as a result of the contact with the West, untouchability has been abolished and caste no longer is king in India. . . . There is no doubt, therefore, that the changes that have been brought about in Asian life by the contact with Europe are radical and far-reaching, and will not disappear as many observers are inclined to think with the rise of a new Asian sentiment.

It would be useful at this point to examine the major features where Western influences are likely to be permanent, and the extent of these influences on Asian societies in general.

The first and perhaps the most abiding influence is in the sphere of law. In all Asian countries the legal systems have been fundamentally changed and reorganized according to the post-revolutionary conceptions of nineteenth-century Europe. The first country in which this change was introduced was India where, under the influence of Thomas Babington Macaulay, new legal principles were systematically introduced and applied. I may quote here what I have written elsewhere in this connection: "The legal system under which India has lived for a hundred years and within whose steel frame her social, political and economic development has taken place, is the work of Macaulay. . . . The establishment of the great principle of equality of all before law in a country where under the Hindu doctrines a Brahmin could not be punished on the evidence of a Sudra, and even punishments varied according to caste, and where, according to Muslim law, testimony could not be accepted against a Muslim, was itself a legal revolution of the first importance. Few, indeed, who compare Macaulay's code with its great predecessors, whether those of Manu, Justinian or Napoleon, will cavil at the claim that the Indian penal code was a great improvement on the previous systems."

The imposing and truly magnificent legal structure, under which the 483 million people of India, Pakistan and Burma have lived during the last 100 years, has changed the basis of society in a manner which few people realize. Though the personal laws of different communities may be different, the penal law is the same for all. This has been supplemented by a vast corpus of legislation, which has profoundly affected every kind of social relationship. The position of women in India, for example, has undergone changes which Hindu thought even fifty years ago would have considered revolutionary. Even the personal law of the Hindus, in respect of their succession, inheritance, marriage, joint family and the set of what may be called their special social organization, has been greatly modified by the legal systems now in force in India. There can be no going back on this — in any case to the old Hindu ideas. The transformation brought about by the new legal doctrines of the West is a permanent one and is likely to outlast the more spectacular changes in many other fields. . . .

It is not possible to speak with the same certainty about the political and social structures brought about as a result of the conflict with Europe. The forms of Government, the nature of political rights, democracy in its widest sense, local and municipal administrations — these may all disappear, change their character or survive only in attenuated and unrecognizable forms in certain areas. And yet at the present time they constitute the most spectacular change in Asia. No country in the East is now governed under a system of "Oriental Despotism.". . . India, Burma, Indonesia and China, seats of ancient empires and kingdoms, are all now republican governments. It may be a temporary phase, for no political system can be considered permanent. But it is fairly certain that even if democratic institutions in Asia, as in some Latin American Republics, get metamorphosed into something quite different from their original shape and form, or do not develop in the spirit of genuine vigour, the principles of "Oriental despotism" will not come back. "Oriental despotism" has at all times reflected certain ideas and principles accepted generally by the people. Those ideas and principles no longer find any acceptance. Once the thread is broken the *mystique* of the doctrine also ceases.

So, while the new democratic institution in Asia may not last beyond a few generations or may become transformed quite early into replicas of Liberian democracy, it would yet be true to say that the principles of government that Asia has accepted from the West constitute a major and qualitative change whose influence will penetrate far into the future. The new social structure has to be reflected in new political institutions. Further, the commercial economy resulting in the participation in world trade; industrialization, bringing along with it both the power of accumulated wealth and of organized labour; the growth of organized city life, different from that of the great capital towns of the past; all these, and numerous other factors, render a reversion to the old political structures, based as they were on a rural economy and on land tax, altogether out of the question. No doubt the political structure of Asian countries, though they may now copy the institutions of the West, may in time evolve their own patterns which may not too closely follow the traditions of Europe. But any return to a purely Asian tradition is ruled out by the growth of social, economic and political forces which no country in Asia had to deal with in the past.

The growth of great cities, themselves centres of political and economic dynamism, is a result of European contacts, the immense significance of which has not been fully appreciated. There was a great urban life and culture previous to the arrival of Europeans in India, China and Japan. The very word *nagarika*, a town-dweller, meant a man of sophisticated culture and refined tastes, and has been used in that sense from at least the third century B.C. Great towns like Benares, Pravag, Broach and Surat, unconnected with courts and kings, have flourished in India through historical times. But in general they represented neither political nor municipal life. The *nagarika* did not convey the meaning of citizen. The towns and cities in India, when they were not great capitals, were merely great centres of population, sometimes important from the point of view of trade, often from the point of view of religious sanctity. They did not involve any civic tradition. The same was the case in China.

The new cities, which grew up as a result of European contacts, Bombay, Calcutta and Madras, Shanghai, Tientsin, Singapore, Colombo, Jakarta, etc., represent a new principle: the organization of the city as an independent unit. In Madras, Calcutta and Bombay we have the full paraphernalia of European city life, with sheriffs, mayors, corporations and aldermen. . . .

It is the city that has created the wealthy middle classes in India, China and other Asian countries. The emergence of the middle classes both as leaders in political and economic life and as reservoirs of essential scientific skills, has been in the main the outcome of the new life in the cities. The possibility of the great cities surviving as centres of civilization, even if regression sets in elsewhere inside the countries of Asia much in the same way as in medieval Europe, cannot be overlooked, and if that happens the credit for the survival of the new life in the great cities will certainly belong to Europe.

Another point, one which arises directly out of Europe's long domination over Asia, is the integration of vast territories into great nation States of a kind unknown in the previous history of Asia. India, for instance, all through her long history, had never been welded together into a single State as she is now. Her territorial unity was in the past emphasized by the unity of Hinduism, by the similarity of Sanskrit culture and by a political impulse which led every leading Empire in India to undertake the task of conquering and bringing under one dominion the territory extending from the Himalayas to Cape Comorin. This relentless urge moved every dynasty of importance in the past; but it was never realized.

Even under the British, vast areas, amounting to nearly two-fifths of the territory of India, were under the rule of semi-independent princes. For the first time in history, India has been integrated into a single State living under the same constitution and subject to the same laws. Unquestionably this was the result of a hundred years of British administration which imposed a unity on the peoples of India, both by the machinery of Government which it created and by the forces of resistance to which it gave rise. . . .

So far we have discussed the changes in the social and political institutions which arose directly from Asia's contact with Europe. A vaster and perhaps more significant change is in the realm of ideas, which it is not possible to discuss in this treatise. What the introduction of modern sciences, history and wider knowledge of the world has done to the mind of Asia is a supremely fascinating subject of inquiry. What the outcome of that fermentation will be no one is yet in a position to foresee or forecast. Obviously, it has affected every aspect of life, religion, arts, language, processes of thinking and speculative philosophies which had long held sway over the minds of men. If the Eastern religions and philosophies have not been displaced, and in fact are stronger today, it does not mean that they have not undergone profound changes. As against other religions and other philosophies they have more than held their own; but they have also had to undergo subtle transformations to resolve the conflicts which modern science, more than rival religions, forced on them. Thus the new interpretations of Buddhism and Hinduism reflect in a large measure the influence of modern ideas, mostly arising from contact with Europe.

Philosophy and religious thinking, however much they may influence the people in general, are the special interests of the intellectuals. But not so the language, and it is here that the influence of Europe has been most noticeable. From the great literatures of China, India and Japan to the minor languages spoken only by a few million people, everywhere the influence of the West overshadows past traditions. . . .

In the great languages of India there was at first no revolutionary break with the past. In fact, till about 1914, though the Western forms of writing had taken deep root in the languages, and novels, short stories and dramas were popular and had gained a hold on the public mind, it was the classical tradition that was still dominant. In poetry especially, India, with its 3,000 years of literary inheritance, clung to the forms and manner of Sanskrit classicism, modified to a great extent by the literary renaisssance of the Middle Ages. Even in Tagore, a true product of Victorian culture, the dominance of Sanskrit traditions was clearly visible. He used every known Western form: drama, short story, lyrical poetry, essay; but the voice that spoke was of one nurtured on the epics of Vyasa and Valmiki, the poetry of Kalidasa and Jayadeva and the songs of Vidyapathi, Kabir and Mira. During the last thirty years, however, the literatures of the great Indian languages have undergone a revolutionary change. They are no longer concerned with the refine-

ments of classical style. They borrow freely from all the literatures of the West, the drama from Ibsen, Shaw, Pirandello and Chekhov, the short story and the novel from their French and Russian masters, and poetry from the latest schools in Europe. No longer have they any concern with the lotus and the moon, the swans, the *chatakas* and other time-worn symbolisms of the past.

The new art forms, especially in prose, owe little or nothing to the earlier Indian traditions. It may in fact be said that the thought of Europe is at last being acclimatized in India by the popular literature of the last quarter of a century. The social and political content of the new writing is essentially cosmopolitan, influenced widely by the breakdown of the old society in Europe and by the dynamism of Marxist thought in the widest sense. Also it is not only through literature in its creative aspect that this message is being spread. Weeklies, magazines, newspapers, cinema films and radio constitute the ever-widening popularity of the new literature. . . . It is the New Life — not Europe — that finds its voice echoed in a thousand mouths.

This, few will deny, widens every day the gulf between the past and the present in Asia. It is the change in the language that is in many ways the most far-reaching transformation in Asia, for it is not merely the reflection of the changed mind but is in itself the instrument of continuing changes, for the new languages of Asia represent a new semantics, a new world of ideas and thought which is reaching a larger and larger circle every day. It is significant to note that an immense development of broadcasting was one of the first things that every new State in Asia took in hand after it achieved its independence and, significantly, too, India, China and Indonesia have embarked on a policy of developing their national literatures in order to make them capable of popularizing modern ideals.

It should, however, be emphasized that the increasing acceptance of new ideas, though generated by contact with the West and of late greatly influenced by the October Revolution and the prestige of Communist thought, does not involve a break in the continuity of the great Asian civilizations. The Chinese, Indian and other civilizations, though modified by new ideas and enriched by new experience, continue even in an increasing degree to emphasize their special characteristics. . . . The failure of the Christian attack on Hinduism, Buddhism and, of course, Islam, left them stronger and more vigorous as a result of the adjustments they were called upon to effect. . . . Thus, though the influence of Europe and the penetration of new ideas have introduced vast changes in Asia, and may lead to even greater changes, Asian civilizations will continue to develop their marked individuality and remain spiritually and intellectually separate from Christian Europe.

One strange aspect of Asian political conception which it took a long time to change was the conviction, in India and China especially, that the world outside did not matter. The average Hindu did not know of the existence of countries and peoples outside India. Europe became real to him only in the nineteenth century after the British had established dominion over India. Two wars had to be fought before the Chinese could think of European nations as anything more than barbarian tribes occupying the outer regions of civilization. . . .

It was only during the second half of the nineteenth century that the Asian peoples awoke to the fact that Asia was only a part — and by no means the most important then — of a greater world of which previously they had no knowledge. Gradually the picture became clear to them, first to the Japanese and slowly to the others. The growth of Asia's importance in the twentieth century as a result of the demand for tropical materials, and the emergence of Japan as a great Power and the gradual transformation of China, first as a playground of European rivalries and later as a danger spot, led naturally to a greater realization of Asia's role. After the First Great War, when the leadership of the West passed to America, which unlike European States is also a Pacific Power, Asia was brought more directly into the whirlpool of world politics.

The new Asian States, therefore, can no longer revert to a policy of isolation or pretend ignorance of the existence of other countries. China, India and Indonesia — apart, of course, from Japan — have therefore no mean roles to fill in the politics of the present-day world. That arises directly from the transformation caused by Europe's former Empires over the East.

The effects of Asian contacts on Europe, though considerably less, cannot be considered insignificant. The growth of capitalism in the seventeenth, eighteenth and nineteenth centuries, in itself a profound and revolutionary change, is intimately connected with the expansion of European trade and business into Asia. The political development of the leading Western European nations during this period was also related to their exploitation of their Asian possessions and the wealth they derived from the trade with and government of their Eastern dependencies. Their material life, as reflected in clothing, food, beverages, etc., also bears permanent marks of their Eastern contacts. . . .

Also, archaeology has seriously affected the faith which was so firmly held in the past that everything of value developed on the shores of the Mediterranean. The past of the Great Asian peoples has gradually come to be considered as part of the general heritage of civilized man, and this may in time lead to a breakdown of the narrow Europeanism, which considered everything outside the experience of the West as of secondary importance. These subjects are merely alluded to here to indicate that the influence of the contacts between Asia and Europe is not wholly one-sided and that now, since the political domination of Asia is a thing of the past, the results of the interpenetration of culture may be even more fruitful.

SUGGESTIONS FOR ADDITIONAL READING

This brief bibliographical discussion makes no pretense at a comprehensive survey of historical writing on British rule in India, but is limited to those works which seem most relevant to the problem of arriving at an evaluation of that rule. The student should be warned that the existing literature on the British period in Indian history, despite its bulk, is disappointing in many respects. Historians have yet to achieve a consensus on many aspects of Western history, but they do have the advantage of numerous detailed monographic studies upon which to draw. For Indian history, such detailed investigations are few and far between. Many problems of critical importance in the interpretation of British rule have yet to receive the kind of study which would make possible a satisfactory reappraisal of the themes in dispute in the selections in this volume.

It was perhaps inevitable that the views of British and of Indian writers should diverge sharply in the period prior to the achievement of independence, for then any attempt to analyze the nature and effects of British rule had inescapable political implications. To a considerable degree, however, these same contrasts in interpretation have persisted in the post-independence period. One of the most disconcerting features of much of this literature is the extent to which the partisans of the British and the Indian nationalist viewpoints respectively have failed to communicate with each other. As Robert I. Crane observes in his excellent bibliographical pamphlet, *The History of India: Its Study and Interpretation* (Washington: Service Center for Teachers of History, 1958), "they spoke from different viewpoints, they misunderstood each other's motives, and what seemed self-evident to the one seemed absurd to the other."

Several useful studies devoted specifically to the problem of evaluating British rule have not been included in this booklet, either because they do not easily lend themselves to condensation or because the interpretations they offer are generally similar to those represented among the foregoing selections. One of the most important of these is Sir Percival Griffiths, *The British Impact on India* (London, 1952). Though it is undeniably pro-British in outlook, unlike many such works it does give serious consideration to important themes in the nationalist critique. Another worthwhile study, reflecting the more moderate view of British rule which some Indian writers have taken in the years since independence, is N. V. Sovani, "The British Impact on India before 1850–57," *Journal of World History*, I (1953–54), 857–882, and "The British Impact on India after 1850–57," *ibid.*, II (1954–55), 77–105.

Two good general interpretations are T. Walter Wallbank, *A Short History of India and Pakistan* (New York, 1958), which is available in an inexpensive paperback edition; and Percival Spear, *India, Pakistan, and the West* (London, 1949). A major interpretive effort from an Indian viewpoint is Tara Chand, *A History of the Freedom Movement in India* (vol. I; New Delhi, 1961). It is planned in three volumes, of which only the first, covering the period from the beginning of British rule to the Indian Mutiny of 1857, has yet appeared. An excellent brief summary by Daniel and Alice Thorner constitutes the India section of Ralph Linton (ed.), *Most of the World* (New York, 1949), pp. 549–653. An article by Robert I. Crane, "India: A Study of the Impact of Western Civilization," *Social Education*, XV (Dec., 1951), 365–371, gives a perceptive view of the process of social change in India under British rule.

All of the works from which excerpts have been drawn for this booklet are well worth reading in full. Those of most general interest, however, probably are Jawaharlal Nehru, *The Discovery of India*

(New York, 1946); Sir Reginald Coupland, *The Indian Problem* (3 vols.; London, 1942–43) and *India: A Re-statement* (London, 1945); R. Palme Dutt, *India Today* (Bombay, 1949); L. S. S. O'Malley (ed.), *Modern India and the West: A Study in the Interaction of Their Civilizations* (London, 1941); W. Norman Brown, *The United States and India and Pakistan* (Cambridge, Mass., 1953); and K. M. Panikkar, *Asia and Western Dominance: A Survey of the Vasco Da Gama Epoch of Asian History, 1498–1945* (London, 1959). The volume by Nehru is available in abridged form in a paperback edition.

Among general political histories, the following will be found useful: Edward Thompson and G. T. Garratt, *Rise and Fulfillment of British Rule in India* (London, 1934); R. C. Majumdar, H. C. Raychaudhuri, and K. Datta, *An Advanced History of India* (London, 1960); W. H. Moreland and A. C. Chatterjee, *A Short History of India* (London, 1957); Vincent Smith, *Oxford History of India* (3rd ed., Oxford, 1958, revised by Percival Spear); and Percival Spear, *India: A Modern History* (Ann Arbor, 1961). Philip Woodruff (pseudonym of Philip Mason), *The Men Who Ruled India*, vol. I, *The Founders*, and vol. II, *The Guardians* (London, 1953–54), covers the two centuries of British rule.

The student who wishes to follow the evolution of the nationalist argument should consult Dadabhai Naoroji, *Poverty of India* (London, 1878) and *Poverty and un-British Rule in India* (London, 1901); Romesh Dutt's two-volume *Economic History of India* (London, 1901–03); and Lala Lajpat Rai, *Young India* (New York, 1916) and *England's Debt to India* (New York, 1917), as well as more recent works. Some notable examples of works by Englishmen who were sharply critical of British rule are F. J. Shore, *Notes on Indian Affairs* (2 vols.; London, 1837); William Digby, *'Prosperous' British India: A Revelation from Official Records* (London, 1901); Sir Henry Cotton, *New India, or India in Transition* (London, 1907); and Reginald Reynolds, *White Sahibs in India* (London, 1946). On the other side, the benefits of British rule are stressed by Sir William W. Hunter, *The India of the Queen, and Other Essays* (London, 1903); Sir John Strachey, *India: Its Administration and Progress* (London, 1903); Sir Valentine Chirol, *India* (London, 1926); and Sir John Cumming (ed.), *Modern India: A Co-operative Survey* (London, 1931).

Two basic works for the study of Indian nationalism are Bruce T. McCully, *English Education and the Origins of Indian Nationalism* (New York, 1940), and A. R. Desai, *Social Background of Indian Nationalism* (Bombay, 1959). Sir Verney Lovett, *A History of the Indian Nationalist Movement* (London, 1920) and C. F. Andrews and G. Mukerji, *The Rise and Growth of the Congress in India* (London, 1938) are concerned with the early development of nationalism. S. C. Bose, *The Indian Struggle, 1920–1934* (London, 1935) and Jawaharlal Nehru, *Toward Freedom* (New York, 1941) cover the noncooperation movements of the interwar period; William R. Smith, *Nationalism and Reform in India* (New Haven, 1938) is also useful for this period. The official *History of the Indian National Congress* is by B. Pattabhi Sitaramayya (2 vols.; Madras, 1935–47). Maulana Abul Kalam Azad, *India Wins Freedom* (New York, 1960) is an autobiographical account by a prominent Muslim leader of the Congress. Louis Fischer, *The Life of Mahatma Gandhi* (New York, 1950) will serve as an introduction to this complex figure. Michael Brecher, *Nehru: A Political Biography* (London, 1959) and Hector Bolitho, *Jinnah, Creator of Pakistan* (London, 1954) are both important.

A balanced discussion of the tangled problem of Hindu-Muslim relations is W. Norman Brown, "India's Pakistan Issue," *Proceedings of the American Philosophical Society*, XCI (April, 1947), 162–180. A. Mehta and A. Patwardhan, *The Communal Triangle in India* (Allahabad, 1942) and Rajendra Prasad, *India Divided* (Bombay, 1946) are sharply critical of what they consider British "divide-and-rule" tactics. B. R. Ambedkar, *Pakistan, or the Partition of India* (Bombay, 1946) is favorable to partition, as is Richard Symonds, *The Making of Pakistan* (London, 1950).

There is no satisfactory general economic history of India for the British period; the existing literature is surveyed in Morris D. Morris and Burton Stein, "The Economic History of India: A Bibliographic Essay," *Journal of Economic History*, XXI (June, 1961), 179–207. Some of the more useful works are D. H. Buchanan, *The Development of Capitalist Enterprise in India* (New York, 1934); L. C. A. Knowles, *The Economic Development of the British Overseas Empire*, vol. I (London, 1924); Vera Anstey, *Economic Development of India* (London, 1952); and D. R. Gadgil, *The Industrial Evolution of India* (London, 1944). Two significant articles by Daniel Thorner are "Great Britain and the Development of India's Railways, 1849–1947," *Journal of Economic History*, XI (Fall, 1951), 389–402, and "Pattern of Railway Development in India," *Far Eastern Quarterly*, XIV (Feb., 1955), 201–216. Daniel and Alice Thorner, *Land and Labour in India* (Bombay, 1962) is a collection of important but specialized articles. M. L. Darling, *The Punjab Peasant in Prosperity and Debt* (London, 1925) is a classic account. An older work, A. Loveday, *The History and Economics of Indian Famines* (London, 1914) is still valuable. A detailed statement of the nationalist critique of British fiscal policy is given in Indian National Congress, *Report [of the Select Committee on the Financial Obliga-*

tions between Great Britain and India] (2 vols.; Bombay, 1931); a shorter account is J. C. Kumarappa, *Public Finance and Our Poverty: The Contribution of Public Finance to the Present Economic State of India* (Ahmedabad, 1945).

In recent years, a number of valuable specialized scholarly studies have begun to appear. Among them may be noted Holden Furber, *John Company at Work* (Cambridge, Mass., 1948); Kenneth Ballhatchet, *Social Policy and Social Change in Western India, 1817–1830* (London, 1957); Sarvepalli Gopal, *The Viceroyalty of Lord Ripon, 1880–1884* (London, 1953), and *The Viceroyalty of Lord Irwin, 1926–1931* (Oxford, 1957); Eric Stokes, *The English Utilitarians and India* (Oxford, 1959); B. B. Misra, *The Indian Middle Classes: Their Growth in Modern Times* (London, 1961); George D. Bearce, *British Attitudes towards India, 1784–1858* (New York, 1961); and Robert A. Huttenback, *British Relations with Sind, 1799–1843: An Anatomy of Imperialism* (Berkeley, 1962). Scholarly articles on Indian history unfortunately are still far too rare in American and British historical journals. Some excellent recent examples, however, are Thomas R. Metcalf, "The Influence of the Mutiny of 1857 on Land Policy in India," *The Historical Journal*, IV (1961), 152–163; J. Duncan M. Derrett, "The Administration of Hindu Law by the British," *Comparative Studies in Society and History*, IV (Nov., 1961), 10–52, and J. H. Broomfield, "The Vote and the Transfer of Power: A Study of the Bengal General Election, 1912–1913," *Journal of Asian Studies*, XXI (Feb., 1962), 163–181.